Numerology

You Need to Become a Master Numerologist

(How to Embrace the Synchronicities of Angel Numbers)

Everett Buck

Published By **Tyson Maxwell**

Everett Buck

Numerology: You Need to Become a Master Numerologist (How to Embrace the Synchronicities of Angel Numbers)

ISBN   978-1-998038-00-8

No part of this guidebook shall be reproduced in any form without permission in writing from the publisher except in the case of brief quotations embodied in critical articles or reviews.

Legal & Disclaimer

The information contained in this book is not designed to replace or take the place of any form of medicine or professional medical advice. The information in this book has been provided for educational & entertainment purposes only.

The information contained in this book has been compiled from sources deemed reliable, and it is accurate to the best of the Author's knowledge; however, the Author cannot guarantee its accuracy and validity and cannot be held liable for any errors or omissions. Changes are periodically made to this book. You must consult your doctor or get professional medical advice before using any of the suggested remedies, techniques, or information in this book.

Table Of Contents

Chapter 1: How do you define numerology?

Let's begin this guide into the realm of numerology with the basics of what is numerology.

Numerology is the field that investigates the relationship between a person's birth date and full name, along with the person's personal life and character.

It's an intriguing discipline which is thought to have its roots in the time of ancient Greece and is believed to have been created by Pythagoras of Samos although there's no evidence to support this.

Pythagoras is most well-known for his Pytaghorean Theorem and his mathematical philosophy as well as for his idea of metempsychosis.

Which of these concepts are essential for understanding the discipline of numerology?

In order to answer this question, it is essential to provide details about the fundamental figures for Pythagoras.

In the time of Greece the most popular topic for speculation was the question about the Ark of life , and for the founder of numerology, it was the most important number to be in this place, meaning that he believed that it was the central point of the universe and the source of its existence. Everything that is derived from numbers could be tracked back to a specific number.

It is also crucial to understand what metempsychosis means that is the concept of immortality for soul and the possibility of its transmigration from one body to the next.

Numerology is deeply linked with the concept of the number as the ark of life as well as metempsychosis is a concept, therefore it is crucial to keep both in your mind.

Like I said earlier, numerology is a study of the relationship of numbers and birth names to the person's life and character.

It's about an interaction, a connection between these two things, which is totally unrelated.

It's impossible to know how closely they are connected to one another or how they could be connected in this manner, but that's exactly what numerology is all about.

There's a mystery in this field, and it is it is a baffling one.

The mystery is created because of the reality that numerology readings actually work, but without any rational explanation.

When the first time one receives an entire and well-constructed reading, it is a time of change in the individual's life, triggered by a shock that is first experienced; however, nobody is willing to acknowledge that a field of study referred to as "pseudoscience" can really function.

However, following the shock, there's a period of time to process the new information that will lead to a completely fresh and new method of comprehending oneself.

There is an undercurrent genius to the development of this field, an concept that was thought up by someone possibly Pythagoras and eventually worked.

This subject is something that our human understanding cannot even begin to explain.

Mendel as an example, analyzed the inheritance laws and described what he saw in crossings of seeds However, he wasn't able to tell anything about how they occurred because he did not know any of the workings of DNA or genes. He just expressed what he saw, and believed it to be real.

In numerology, perhaps one could say that somehow some person from the past period of time was able to describe something with an intuition, but did not know what or why.

Today, we aren't able to pinpoint the reason or how however, we can observe that it is working.

Maybe, just maybe, numerology is not a complete "pseudoscience" but just a aspect of reality that cannot be explained.

Chapter 2: The energy of Number

Numerology is founded by nine numbers also known as units, and the relation between these numbers and the name of the person and their date of birth, which creates your numerological charts.

There are many methods of counting numbers, and each one has a particular meaning that corresponds to the personality of the individual.

When discussing the numbers within this field, he must speak about energy. This involves a slight change in the way that one thinks about the world and experience it. It is evident that one typically thinks in terms of material as that's what we perceive and feel, however, when one begins to study this field, he must consider the world in terms of energyand change his perspective to shift the way of thinking about things beyond just the senses and seeing instead of what you feel, as well as what one can imagine.

The ability to feel and be intuitive is essential to the understanding of numerology and the notion of energy that numbers carry.

Number 1

One is regarded as to be the initiater.

It is a symbol of the first, the first to arrive or the one who is the winner. The source of this energy is the feeling of self-worth that is at the heart of the power of the number.

Number 2

The two represents the opposite of the energy of one. It symbolizes the relationship between a couple, of two persons, acquaintances and partners, mother and son father and son siblings, brothers and so on.

It's the desire to form a bond and the desire to meet the person who is not there.

Number 3

The three is the collective energy. It's the social aspect of human beings, the potential to build an entire society.

Number 4

The power of # 4 represents the desire to create new structures, new organizations and then to guide them with discipline and order to ensure they last over time.

Number 5

It's the enthusiasm of excitement. The human instinct within is to explore new ideas and uncovering new realities in the world.

Number 6

Six energy represents the medical energy, the power of the treatment.

Number 7

This is the power of wisdom that is the result of consciousness and understanding.

Number 8

The energy of the number 8 is one of rule, of sovereignty and supremacy. It is a symbol of power as well as justice, law and money.

Number 9

This is the power that is liberation, mission, diplomacy as well as inspiration, political as well as civil rights.

It is the connection between these energies within a numerological chart which creates the persona of a person, therefore the numbers aren't fixed and static However, they mix with one another, creating an individual and distinct persona, even if they remain in the same order to keep their unique impact on the individual. It is important to look at how they function together and how they affect one another, and observing the effects on a person's life. This is the reason why each numerological chart is unique from the next.

Chapter 3: Destiny Number

The number of destiny is undoubtedly the key number that defines a person's life, and also the number which people typically feel the bond.

It's the energy which comes out of the theosophical total of numbers that compose the birth date.

Example:

12/03/1995

=> 12: 1+2 = 3

=> 3

=> 1995: 1 + 9 + 9 + 5= 24 => 2+4 = 6

The numbers have to be returned into one group.

The final paragraph is the sum of the three results previously obtained:

=> 3 + 3 + 6 = 12 => 1 + 2 = 3

In this case, the number for destiny is 3.

As we've learned previously the three's energy is one that is shared by the social group, or of life. Anyone who is blessed with it will be a person who communicates, who lives the life of a group, and also has creative skills.

This isn't a general fact, since people could form the center of a group, but they could also be the most attractive ones, and be innovative or not. For those who don't have these characteristics such as a 3 in the numerological chart would not be very helpful.

The destiny number is the basis of a person's character and her main characteristics. However it also provides details on who the individual will be in the future which is why it's called a destiny number. This is because it describes the reason the person was born on this earth.

Chapter 4: Life journey

Life path number serves similar functions to destiny number, however, there's a difference.

The number "destiny" talks about life generally Life number speaks directly about the potential career path the person should pursue.

There is a possibility to say that the life journey will be more focused on what a person is destined to accomplish during this life, whereas destiny numbers are more about who the person was supposed to be.

It is estimated by adding of the letters of the surname and name together.

To determine which number is related to the particular letter, there is a correspondence comprised of letters and numbers.

It's also known as"the numerological alphabet.

1 2 3 4 5 6 7 8 9

A B C D E F G H I

J K L M N O P Q R

S T U V W X Y Z

Example:

Mary Smith:

4197 14928

=> 4 + 1 + 9 + 7 = 21 => 2 + 1 = 3

=> 1 + 4 + 9 + 2 + 8 = 24 => 2 + 4 = 6

=> 3 + 6 = 9

Chapter 5: Soul number, personality and mature

Soul number

It's also referred to as heart's desire because it expresses the most fundamental needs of a person.

It's the number assigned to a soul, and it's reflected its frequency.

It's something that is gone from the present and provides information on the incarnated part of self, the immortal self.

The total of the vowels in the name determines the heart's desire number.

Example:

Mary Smith

1 7. 9

Sum:

=> 1 + 7 = 8

=> 9

=> 8 + 9 = 17 => 1 + 7 = 8

Mary Smith's heart's desire for Mary Smith is 8.

Personality number

It is used to describe a person's character or the traits of someone and the manner in which an individual displays on the outside.

It's essentially disguised as a social one. It can be determined by adding consonants of name and surname , and then using the same numerals.

The number of the maturity

It's the amount of a person's development.

It describes how the person's growth will be and what their life when they reach 30 will be similar to. It is about a person's realization and this is the reason why it's also referred to as the realization number or number of the ultimate.

To calculate it , simply add the destiny number to life path.

In the same scenario:

Destiny number 3

Life Path 9

Quintessence: 3 + 9 = 12 => 1 + 2 = 3

The number of maturity, similar to the life path numbers, can help someone determine their ideal path to a career.

Chapter 6: The explanation for the number

As I mentioned earlier When one is thinking about numbers in numerology , one should think of them as energies or vibrations that affect the lives of people.

It can be extremely useful to imagine the archetypes of these characters.

An archetype is the very first absolute and autonomous example.

This is an unique image that is found inside the collective subconscious, which was developed by psychoanalyst Carl Gustav Jung. Jung studied many archetypes, and described them as inner concepts that organize information according to certain models.

This is exactly what numerology is all about: numbers as predetermined models on which the mind and knowledge create themselves.

In this book, the numbers are not seen as archetypes of Jung, rather as Key Words, as archetypes for the ideas behind each number.

Number 1 Combativity

The number 1 is described as the strength in the fight, the one who is first and is the one who wins.

It is the power of autonomy, independence, self-construction, self work Self centrality, self-reliance.

The warrior is a part of self-control, it's the increase in capacity, strength to self-power, self-made concepts, and self-power.

Key Words: Combativity, Self, Independence, Freelance, Victory, Initiative, Activity, Leadership.

Number 2 Innocence

It is also known as the energy of innocence, or the childhood energy. It's the energy of tenderness friendship, kindness, and compassion, that is why the energy is an absorbing energy which permits first place to be first.

The first makes the decision and the other takes the decision. The second is also the relationship with another and the human desire to be in an intimate relationship. It serves the other. It's a sweet and uplifting energy.

Key words: innocence, Kindness, Kindness Innocence, Passivity, Caring, Love, Relationship.

Number 3 Entertainment

The number 3 represents the group, and in reality it is the combination of three parts, or three elements. It is symbolized by the jester. It is the essence of a gathering, the center of a group, the one who keeps live the party and is always seeking to be noticed. In the end, it's all about communicating.

Keywords: entertainment Sociality, Groups Fun, Communication Expression and Creativity. Beauty and Sensuality. Show, Writing.

Number 4 Constructiveness

It is the power of the construction worker and the builder, who naturally can vary between people in a myriad of areas. The 4 energy is responsible for organizing and building his work, it is a real energy closely linked to earth and matter. This is the power of order and order.

Keywords: Constructiveness Organization order, Categorization Architecture, Structure Earth, Materialism, Practicality Thinking.

Number 5 Research

The 5 energy is the spirit of the seeker, of the seeker, of the desire to discover and discover new life secrets as well as new laws and truths. There is also the desire to seek out new ways to be fully present in life in order to experience every emotion and sensations it provides.

It's an identification number for the seeker the experienced, of the traveler and adventurer.

Key words: Research Adventure Travel, Discover Passion, Desire Intelligence, Curiosity, Sensuality, Experience, Liberty and Creativity.

Number 6 Love

Sixth number reflects the power that a Guardian Angel has. the power of security and custody, as well as caring for. It's the arm over the shoulders, or the hug when you are in a crisis or the need for medicine from the physician, and the tenderness and concern of the mother. It is the sound of family, weddings as well as friendship, loyalty, and traditions. It also has plenty of energy for imaginative activities that offer benefit to anyone, such as gardening, restoration as well as psychotherapy, animal care, and medicine.

Key Words: Love Motherhood, Care Fatherhood, Brotherhood, Friendship Beauty, Art and Restoration, as well as and advice.

Number 7 Wisdom

The 7 energy symbolizes wisdom, knowledge and high consciousness. It is a vibration of discernment, intelligence, as well as constructive critique. It is manifested in science, the arts, and mysticism. It is a pulsating sound when studying reading, silence, and reading. It also symbolizes the mentor's guidance and advice.

Key Words: Wisdom, Intelligence, Professionality, Experience, Study, Curiosity, Science, Spirituality, Mysticism,

Critic, Intuition, Music, Creativity.

Number 8 Sovereignty

The energy of the 8 can be used to refer to one who is sovereign. The regal and noble. It is a symbol of strength, power and wealth, it is also referred to as abundance. It has the power of law and justice. It is a symbol of entrepreneurship and stock exchanges.

Key words: Sovereignty, Power, Richness, Abundance, Money, Nobility, Justice, Law, Leadership.

Number 9 Mission

The number 9 represents the spirit of the liberator as well as the missionary. It has the power that is associated with civil rights and the person who is open-minded and does not judge that is based on superficial or ad hoc beliefs. A person with this type of energy is free from prejudices and a defender for equality and justice. It is an evangelist who goes around across the globe to assist children and those in need and in difficulty. It is the politician, the diplomat and the politician.

The key words are Mission Rights, Justice, Leadership Love, Completion Political Interest, Diplomacy, Liberty.

Chapter 7: Shadows

It is evident that all of these numbers have shadows, meaning that they each have a positive, but also negative energy to the individual's life.

Let's take a look at these shadows , which could be considered archetypes as well.

Number 1 Rebellion

The negative aspect of the first number is symbolized by the act of rebellion. Rebels are the person who refuses to play with the norms of society any longer and begins to become a bit offbeat. The issue with this is the feeling of being the odd one or the other one and the resulting loneliness that is that comes from being not understood.

The rebel could also mean one who is constantly trying to voice his opinion, and not focusing on the opinions of others, and who is constantly fighting and disputing. It is possible that he has difficulty maintaining the peace, and may be too absorbed on himself. He can eventually be the egocentric one, the narcissist with vices like preposterousness and arrogance.

Keywords: rebellion Egocentrism, Narcissism, Intolerance Anger, arrogance Competitiveness.

Number 2 Victimhood

The shadow of the two energy's shadow can be symbolized by the vibrating that an orphan. The term "orphan" refers to someone who has had issues with their parents, and feels a sense of abandonment. He is believed to always in need of attention.

He's like an unending Peter Pan, who doesn't wish to develop yet, on the exact opposite, he'll always wants someone to will take charge of him. He is a child being dependent on another person, usually his parents but sometimes an acquaintance or partner.

An injured child is a sign of disillusioned innocence, which is why they develop a detached and skeptical character. The term "orphan" does not mean an innocent person who helps others, but on the opposite, someone who requires assistance.

Key Words: Victimhood, Needs, Infantilism, Judgment, Touchiness, Dependency.

Number 3 Estrangement

In contrast to the humor energy is the energy of the stranger. The jester is often exaggerated, too extroverted, exaggerated, and too eccentric. The goal of the jester is being the heart of the group and the center of the group. That is the reason he desires to be noticed by others. This could cause him to become too attracted by his appearance.

The stranger should be careful not to be too shallow or too focused on himself or overly eccentric. The stranger must also be cautious about paying the time to show respect to others since he is prone to behave like a bully by highlighting with humor the weaknesses and shortcomings of other people, so as to appear to be the smartest and beautiful and the most likable in general.

Key Words: Estrangement, Dispersivity, Superficiality, Betrayal, Bullying, Exaggeration, Strangeness.

Number 4 Imprisonment

Shadows of builders are that of the prisoner. The most destructive aspect of organization actually is excessive organization that results in rigidity and, ultimately, being stuck in borders and walls erected by the individual. The four are prone to developing an obsessive compulsive disorder getting really angry when the plans he devised are not met or his borders are not respected.

Key Words: Imprisonment, Inflexibility, Compulsion, Obsession, Intolerance, Anger, Despotism.

Number 5 Wandering

A shadow that reflects the seeker's shadow is the rover, who represents the seeker who couldn't find a home to remain. The seeker can get caught up in the pursuit of travel or experiencing through the senses and have issues with drugs, alcohol or nicotine, sexual activities and food. But he could also develop another type of dependence, as the urge to travel or to learn and study could lead to addictions for the number 5.

He could never meet someone who will stay for the duration of their lives and never to make a family or cheat on his partner , which can destroy relationships and families.

Key Words: Wandering, Dependence, Betrayal, Irresponsible.

Number 6 Martyrdom

A martyr can be described as the part that is destructive of the 6th number. In reality, the person who is always looking to give back can be sacrificed in order to help others. The issue with this is that sometimes he could be used by other people. Another disadvantage of those who are martyrs is he gives all of his time to others, never receiving anything back and he may begin to be a victim and engage in victimhood. Additionally, the six is prone to an impression that he is more knowledgeable than others. This could cause him to always seek to win in any argument and always seek to be the best. He frequently gives advice without asking for them and is prone to believe that the best advice is one he is able to give to people who do not follow his suggestions and, most of the time, the six appears to be critical and judgemental.

Key Words: Martyrdom, Judgment, Oppression, Invasion, Touchiness, Arrogance, Victimhood.

Number 7 Isolation

The necessity to be able to study alone can lead to the seven falling into isolation. This is that of the wise, who find themselves isolated from others due to the fact that his expertise isn't common to everyone else and can cause him to feel isolated and unappreciated. The seven is a person with ideals, but the current world isn't built on these ideals and values which is why he may be able to be a lonely person and even put himself on top of the tower for eternity. A further issue is that the seven could really be a critic to people around him since he is smart, the one who has knowledge and wisdom. Therefore, the seven is not able to tolerate human weakness. The seven could easily develop anxiety and depression but he also has numerous physical ailments. In reality, he's a extremely fragile person that can be easily overwhelmed and physically hurt due to stress.

Keywords: isolation isolation, loneliness, judgement Manipulation, Coldness Depression, Lie, Anxiety.

Number 8 Tyranny

The power of the sovereign will be in contrast to the power of the tyrant. It is her destructive side.

The former regent could become a tyrant after being a victim of power and intimidation.

It is important to be extremely cautious as the power of the dictator can be extremely damaging to others One of the most destructive aspects of the general population is not only due to the level of anger that he holds within however, but also due to the power that he holds in his control. In reality, most of the true rulers are represented by this number on their chart of numerological numbers and if they fail to utilize it to their advantage, they will certainly degrade society and those who comprise it.

Another issue with this number is its relationship to money. It's a great number to make money, however, it must be utilized in a proper manner. When the energy is contaminated, it can cause serious damage especially in the economy.

A family tyrant might be a parent who does not take care of children and acts violently at them. Or, the teacher who abuses his power , or even an untrustworthy politician.

It may also be a 'bully' into the classroom.

As a tyrant , he could face a number of difficulties communicating his emotions and feelings which is why he's extremely cold.

Keywords: Tyranny Emotionless, Harshness, Coldness, Despotism, Intolerance, Anger

Narcissism, Egocentrism, Judgment and Bullying.

Number 9 Detachment

An angel of the fallen is the counterpart to the liberator. In this instance the destructive aspect of the energy focuses on the inside of the individual, on how he views the world, and also on his persona or social identity. The person with the energy nine is a person with the highest ideals and values which means that he is able to easily sucked out of the violence of the world. This is why he could be a person who has extreme doubt, raw irony, and detachedness. In the end, he will put aside his belief about the universe.

The key words are: detachment Indifference Coldness, Emotionless Insanity, Harshness, Skepticism, bullying.

Chapter 8: Jobs

There are jobs that are adapted to the particular energy, and here's a quick of a list:

Number 1

freelance. The area in which you freelance is dependent on the energy level of other numbers.

Number 2

In an asylum, working with babies in the nursery. Being a babysitter being a midwife, an midwife. As a secretary in a relationship with a boss. As a health professional as a veterinarian assistant. Cleaning person.

Number 3

working in the field of communication, such as actors, writers or speaker, television host, or journalist. Additionally, they work in the field of beauty or art for example, a choreographer stylist models, beauticians, photographer, and video producer. Public public speaker psychologist of work, sales, persuasion, marketing employee.

Number 4

Management jobs. Secretary jobs, organizational jobs. Also , construction jobs, architectural, geometric as well as pharmacy and chemistry. Also, manual jobs are adapted to the blacksmith, the gardener, the tailor, the proprietor of a shop, or accounting jobs. Good mechanics or engineer, plumber. Forest ranger Military.

Number 5

Esthetic work, jobs that involve the study of beauty. Jobs in the field of art. Scientific research. Reviewer, guide to tours and writer.

Number 6

Psychology, medicine, health healthcare professions. Restoration, gardening, veterinary. Also, housewife or household.

Education jobs, teacher. Social assistant. Trainer and motivator.

Number 7

Professional, specialist researcher, scientist, fields of science and psychology, medicine. Teacher in training. Better freelance. Mystic and occultist. Philosopher.

Number 8

Boss, and even better if you freelance. The job is based on other numbers in the numerological chart. Of course , entrepreneur and investor.

Number 9

Mission, volunteer homes for families, mission. Medicine, psychology, social assistant. Diplomat, politician.

Chapter 9: Numerology and well-being

There is a connection between wellness and numerology, because numerology can be an effective and healing discipline.

The ability to know one's numbers is very beneficial to know more about oneself, and, in a way that is easy to know what makes an individual feel happy and what could cause him to feel terrible.

Numerology is a method to help heal, particularly from a psychological perspective. This is due to the fact that in addition to revealing the strengths of an person, this field can also reveals weaknesses as well as providing suggestions on how one can conquer these weaknesses.

Some people are unable to comprehend the reasons why certain things happen often However, once they have taken into consideration their numerological chart as well as the energy that influences them, their lives change. They are reassured and relieved as they gain insight into the causes of their problems and find peace.

A large number of physical ailments have an emotional root, as they originate from an approach to life that isn't adapted to the individual. The study of numerology may help an individual begin with a fresh way of living and adapting to his character and life way of life. As a result, anxiety and stress are reduced, and the psychosomatic symptoms decrease dramatically.

Numerology also has a connection to the idea of reincarnation, helping people find an entirely new faith in the world and faith in God's power and also to lessen the fear of death that is part of our nature.

Chapter 10: Numbers of Karmic Debt

The numbers for karmic debt are directly linked to the idea of reincarnation which states that the soul travels from one body to another and lives on after the other and in the different lives, she brings with her the consequences of one's actions. This makes one suffer the consequences of their own actions. This is known as Karma and in numerology , it is expressed through the numbers of karmic debt that specifically carry along with them the outcomes of previous life actions.

These numbers are 13, 14, 16 19.

Number 13/4

The number 13 is usually a reference to a previous life that was based on laziness. Other people were working while the individual profited from this. On the other hand to this one must fight and try numerous times to get the things he desires. The main words to remember in this context are constancy and perseverance. The obstacles and challenges will be present in the person's roots even if he puts all his effort into his work. The person must be taught not to quit, but instead to be strong and resilient in the face of any challenges that life throws at him.

Other characteristics are the same as those of 4, with the shadow being underlined and the shadow being more prominent. The main lesson to be learned from this 4 is to discover how to manage his energy in conjunction in the direction of the three that will stop him from become detached and material and incorporating a more joyful and energetic energy. At times, the four could become too rigid within his own frameworks and strategies which is why it is important to take on the energy of the three and discover space for art, feelings and emotions, in addition to the seriousness and hard work as represented by the number four.

Number 14/5

The number 14 refers to a previous existence where the person has over-extended his desire to be free. This implies that he's been through addictions, has been caught cheating numerous times and perhaps with multiple partners, he moved between jobs and the next and was dispersive. and he was a loser. However, it could also be a reference to an earlier life in which the individual's freedom was abused and the individual could be a slave or even a prisoner. This is the reason he doesn't be content with the limitations of his own freedom , and may engage in risky behaviors to maintain his freedom.

Anyone who is in karmic debt must be aware of the risk of develop addiction and engage in a cheating relationship with friends and family members.

Other characteristics are the same as those in 5, with the shadow highlighted and more.

The five needs to learn how to be completely free, without exaggeration, as well as how to create plans and projects using the power of the four without scattering all of its ideas and abilities which is the main problem facing the five.

Number 16/7

The number 16 is a reference to a previous life in which the person wasn't able to handle the power of seven. The person probably utilized his knowledge in a wrong manner and perhaps he hid himself in the tower and shutting himself off from the world. Or perhaps he used it to aid others but instead for the wrong reasons. In addition, it is a reference to cheating on the faith of someone else.

In actual fact this particular number has always encountered issues with trust and faith in his life, and especially when it comes to relationships.

The Karmic number 16 is an ongoing process of tearing everything down and rebuilding everything every day. That is to say, people who are karmic constantly creating chaos in their lives and then rebuilding it and again, which is because they gain knowledge, learn more about the spiritual and conscious at the same time they release their ego.

The 16 is an selfish person that needs to let go of it in order to apply his knowledge to the service of people around him and to serve as a guide and an educator. The 16-year-olds need to rebuild new faith in the universe.

The number seven is a single number. In this case, the number 16/7 it is necessary to learn to combine his seven energy, which can makes him feel isolated and in solitude, along and the six energy that propel him towards building of a family as well as serving other people. In this instance the person has to learn to utilize his expertise and knowledge to aid others.

Number 19/1

The number 19 is a reference to a previous life in which the victim of abuse of his power to his own benefit.

It's about a leader who did not use his position to aid others, but to benefit himself.

The aim of the 19 during this time is to utilize his leadership, as represented by the number 1 in the assistance of others. Number 9 offers the 1 the aspect of charity that leads the 19/10, or 10/1, to take a decision in their lives that is based on helping the society.

19 is also known as "leader of god" because it is a highly spiritual force that has learned how to apply its leadership to serve of humanity in a lively and captivating manner.

Chapter 11: Beginning with one

Beginning with one, numbers must be able to work with the energy of one that is the self's energy. Self-centrality is everywhere that these numbers represent, as well as much ego to tackle. And this isn't just in the case of the numbers deemed as karmic and all the numbers that have number one.

Let's take a look:

Number 11/2

Number 11 must work really hard to develop a sense of self, much more than any other numbers. This is due to the fact that the person is a person with the dual energy of the one, and is both centered and focused on his own. Anyone with this number must be aware of the possibility that this energy could be very destructive if it's not balanced and directed in the correct direction. The best thing for the number 11 is to utilize its great leadership for social causes and to show its artistic talent and to be an expert in the area of beauty or art. A person with the number 11 must give room for spirituality in his life, as without it, he can turn into a real destructive.

Number 12/3

Number 12 is based by utilizing the energy of number 1 as well as number 2. And of course number 3. It is a number that needs to display its artistic and multi-potential aspect without losing its connection to kindness and kindness. One of the issues with three is that the person can be apathetic towards others to attain what they want and the lesson learned in both is focussed on the truth that the three must not neglect to be considerate of other people and treat people with respect. Additionally, the three is an individual who uses his beauty to attract others and thus has numerous partners. The two is the symbol of a couple. Therefore, the three needs to learn to keep expressing his gifts, while participating in various groups, without losing the most intimate relationships that exist in the world. The three is sometimes an unassuming number, whereas the two are compassionate and loving in contrast. In this paradox the 12/3 has a message to be learned for the 12/3. It should be taught to avoid the risk of becoming superficial and materialistic by interacting to the sensitivity of the two energy.

Number 15/6

Number 15/6 should be taught to not over-exaggerate the energy of the number 6, balancing it with the energy of number 5. The number 6 is all about love, family and responsibility, as well as traditional values. That's why for 15/6, there is a need to avoid being too focused on the family, or too accountable and, consequently, too serious. In contrast one hand, the person should let loose the grip to allow the doorway to fun and excitement.

Number 17/8

The number 8 refers to the actual word building, and the need to pay attention to the practical side of our lives. It's the number of business and affairs. In this instance, the seven energy wants the eight to bring together knowledge, wisdom, and spirituality of number seven alongside the practicality and physicality of number 8. However the number eight must pay attention to its own inner wisdom and knowledge to attain great results, or else he is at risk of failing to accomplish anything.

Number 18/9

This number is about taking the idealistic and humanistic characteristics of the nine with the practicality associated with the 8. It provides the mission of the nine opportunity to express itself through the physical concreteness, as it could, for example, manifest itself through the construction of schools for children who are poor or by establishing a charity fund. The main lesson from this nine is learning how to implement his idealistic impulses into action.

Chapter 12: Master numbers

Master numbers are the old souls that have come back to earth to assist humanity in advancing. They are exceptional spiritual entities with a unique gift.

One thing to keep in mind when performing the addition of numbers is that masters should be allowed to make numbers be integers.

For instance If a person was born on the 11th of February, 1995, then the addition will occur using the following method:

Day: 11 not 2

Destiny: 11 + 2 + 6 = 19/1 not 2 + 2 + 6 = 10/1

In this particular case, this case, the number of destiny is symbolized by the number karmic 19/1, and not just by the energy number 1.

These four numbers are the masters:

Number 11: Geniality

Master number eleven will inspire others, since the person who is the ability to inspire and is talented. He's in the position of being the genius, and to make the gap between the visible and invisible world less. They are geniuses in a certain field of study Their strength is intuition , and they are effortlessly spiritual guides.

Number 22: Realization

The energy of 22 is the 4 energy that the builder that is put to the service of others, due to that double-two. This is the power of realizing and the ability to put into action the ideals one has in mind. A person is able to turn his ideas into reality. He is a publicist and can implement public works or develop cutting-edge technology. He's got the ability to leadership and determination. His strength is in creating.

Number 33: Teaching

This is the number that is the master of the master of the universe, also known as the one who is the savior. It is the number that represents the master of communication, therefore those with this number are typically souls who have come to earth to assist others to regain their connection to the spiritual realm through using words. The compassionate one that works in the field of human rights and may be an educator. Master 33 refers to person who is unconditionally loved. His strength is communication.

Number 44: Government

In the case of the 44 energy, you can conclude that the power behind this number is that of the regent master. It's about the one who directs the society towards the proper direction. However, it also represents an energy that is deeply linked to the earth, and the master44 is there to aid those who have earth-related issues as well as material problems. He is an ecologist, a regnant and veterinary professional or biologist, who works to safeguard animals and earth as well as or a dietician. The power of matter.

Chapter 13: For better understanding

A quick chart of numerology

Marilyn Monroe

The birth name is Norma Jeane Mortenson Baker

Birth date 01/06/1926

Day: 1

Destiny: 1 + 6 + 9 = 16/7

Life Path 7+8 + 7 +1 = 23/5

Heart's desire: 7 + 11 + 8 + 6 = 32/5

Personality: 9 + 6 + 8 + 4 = 27/9

Maturity: 7 + 5 = 12/3

Day 1:

Hers was the most gorgeous woman in her day.

- Desire to win

- She developed her own production company

She was the top one beauty model

- A strong sense of Self

Destiny 16/7:

- High intelligence

Feeling lonely

- Want to be with your own

Feeling ununderstood

Try to achieve perfection

- Sophisticated

- Attention to details

Troubled Life

Family concerns

- Sexually sexually

Heart's desire 32/5:

She was a free soul

She had many husbands and partners

She suffered from addictions

The energy of both of them made her appear elegant and soft appearance

The power that the 3 gave her the idea of the star, which was

- Curiosity

- The desire to be adventurous

The desire to live your the life

- Intelligence

Personality 9:

She had a very humane side

She contributed a great deal of money to assist children at in various ways

Chapter 14: Tips and tricks!

Tips and suggestions for the number one spot

Be aware of the way you tend to rule: be aware of your tendencies to rule, which can be exaggerated to the point of absurdity. You may be the intolerant and bully one. Try to be more considerate of others at times and be more friendly.

Beware of loneliness: as one, you are likely to work by yourself. However, this could lead to a total loneliness which isn't good for anyone. Therefore, you should try to show your independence without separating yourself from the rest of the world.

Intimacy: In a relationship you believe you're the right person, and others make mistakes. You should strive being more open in your relationships and try to be more co-operative and open with your spouse.

Job: Try to work as a freelancer and start your own business.

Tips and tricks for the number 2

Self-confidence: strive to maintain your self-confidence, even if you are the other. You may like to hide in the shadows, letting others take the spotlight however this shouldn't be a reason to cause you to feel that you're not as important or insignificant to other people. Your rules are fundamental as you are the roots of the tree.

Avoid victimhood: It is common to appear to be the victim in the event usually when it comes to family, but you may be this way when you are with acquaintances. Be aware that it isn't always the other's blame in the event of a problem and victimhood can create the impression of an unpleasant person. In the end, it's not beneficial for your health.

Relationships: it is important to find an arrangement that allows you to you can best express two energy levels, however, you should be wary of squeezing yourself into a one relationship. There's more to life than just staying at home with a partner and you may suffer from depression if you stay too much in four walls in the same space each day.

Enhance your capacity to take care of others Try to get an employment in the field of health, where you could be of helping other people.

Tips and tips for the number 3

Take note of your tendencies to glamor: you are likely to focus on objects of material and appearance. Be aware that this may cause you to appear too shallow and others will view you in a way that is not appropriate.

Create a strong relationship Try to find an individual you can cherish, even if it seems like you love being the spotlight of many people. It is possible to do this by making a lot of acquaintances and by obtaining jobs that allow for the presence of the public. However, you must ensure that you find someone with whom you have a genuine relationship.

You must work with a crowd communication skill and need to interact with other people. Look for a job that allows you to showcase your creative or artistic skills.

Tips and suggestions for number 4.

Take a step outside of your mind: You tend to get caught up in your logical thinking. This is why it might be beneficial to think outside of your logic, and without placing yourself in danger obviously!

Create plans: you will be able to succeed in making plans for your career and life. This is what you are good at and your forte. Of course , you don't need to overstate your abilities, as you'll also have to make time for relaxation.

It is impossible to manage everything. Not everything can be into your control. Just keep in mind. Sometimes things must be accepted for what they are.

You should try to balance the hours of work and the time for relaxation: you have a tendency to live a sedentary life! Be aware that relaxation is as essential as being productive. You must be in equilibrium, and you cannot simply pick one.

Tips and suggestions for the number 5

Be aware of the things that could make you dependent There are certain things you must manage, particularly like alcohol, nicotine, and food items, and alcohol. There is a higher chance of developing dependence than others.

Travelling can make you feel great. Make time for it.

Study: Find something that catches your interest. You're curious, and should cultivate this curiosity. You can be a successful researcher if you can find something you enjoy in.

Experience: It is important to be having fun and enjoying life and enjoy yourself, that's what you're supposed do. It is essential to experience life and avoid putting yourself in an atmosphere of shyness or avoidance as you'll have many regrets when you get older. Be sure to remember that everything must be done with a sense of balance.

Tips and tips to number 6

Keep your family close: it is important to spend time with your family members, having meals together, participating in things, taking excursions. This is crucial for you. Be sure to take the time to yourself, your family, as well as your significant other.

Create your family. You could be a fantastic parent if you are able to find the right person to start the family you want to have.

Find a way to assist others Consider putting yourself in a social and humane organization, or to find a job that gives you the chance of helping others.

Teaching: You could be an excellent teacher, but you also have to be an excellent coach.

Avoid being a victim: you are likely to act as the victim and blame the problem to others.

Beware of the need to be always the right side of an argument You are the person who is always looking to be right, and cannot think of making mistakes. This isn't true You can't always be right and you need to learn to be open to the opinions of others since everybody has something to learn from. This is a tendency that can cause you to suffer from problems with your family, acquaintances and your partner.

Offer a shoulder people can lean on. You are perfect to be the person whom people can talk to when they're feeling down. Therefore, you must strive to be available whenever people require them. Be aware that some people may profit from your desire to be helpful, and you need to know how to refuse to help.

Tips and tips for number 7

Make time to study If you study you could become an expert in a particular area and it will leave you feeling satisfied.

Be aware of loneliness. You could become a loner If you try to stay away from it!

Avoid harsh criticism. You could be a bit harsh and make people turn out of your way. Use your criticism to benefit others and at the right circumstances.

Do not feel as if you are doing something wrong. If you feel differently, it's because you're different but there's nothing wrong. Your distinctiveness is the reason you are unique and that's exactly the thing that will help you achieve success.

Choose a spiritual competition to keep your faith from fading away in humanity as well as the world at large.

Tips and tricks for number 8

Be patient: Learn become more patient with your family and friends. Be understanding because nobody is perfect, nor you are, and all of us make mistakes from time to time.

Be cautious with your money Don't lose your chance and keep your business secure and well-organized. Be a good business owner as well as a dealmaker and keep even if you fail to succeed the first time around, as you've got the drive to make it in this field.

Expression of emotion: If for you , it's too difficult to express your emotions to the people you feel strongly about, consulting a therapist might be a good idea. It is important to be able to express your emotions and not keep them inside your head otherwise you'll lose connection with them. This can make your family members, and most of all your children be a bit hurt, as the way you express your feelings of love for them can make them believe they don't really love you even a bit.

Number 15/6

Number 15/6 should be taught to not over-exaggerate the energy of the number 6, balancing it with the energy of number 5. The number 6 is all about love, family and responsibility, as well as traditional values. That's why for 15/6, there is a need to avoid being too focused on the family, or too accountable and, consequently, too serious. In contrast one hand, the person should let loose the grip to allow the doorway to fun and excitement.

Number 17/8

The number 8 refers to the actual word building, and the need to pay attention to the practical side of our lives. It's the number of business and affairs. In this instance, the seven energy wants the eight to bring together knowledge, wisdom, and spirituality of number seven alongside the practicality and physicality of number 8. However the number eight must pay attention to its own inner wisdom and knowledge to attain great results, or else he is at risk of failing to accomplish anything.

Number 18/9

This number is about taking the idealistic and humanistic characteristics of the nine with the practicality associated with the 8. It provides the mission of the nine opportunity to express itself through the physical concreteness, as it could, for example, manifest itself through the construction of schools for children who are poor or by establishing a charity fund. The main lesson from this nine is learning how to implement his idealistic impulses into action.

Chapter 15: Master numbers

Master numbers are the old souls that have come back to earth to assist humanity in advancing. They are exceptional spiritual entities with a unique gift.

One thing to keep in mind when performing the addition of numbers is that masters should be allowed to make numbers be integers.

For instance If a person was born on the 11th of February, 1995, then the addition will occur using the following method:

Day: 11 not 2

Destiny: 11 + 2 + 6 = 19/1 not 2 + 2 + 6 = 10/1

In this particular case, this case, the number of destiny is symbolized by the number karmic 19/1, and not just by the energy number 1.

These four numbers are the masters:

Number 11: Geniality

Master number eleven will inspire others, since the person who is the ability to inspire and is talented. He's in the position of being the genius, and to make the gap between the visible and invisible world less. They are geniuses in a certain field of study Their strength is intuition , and they are effortlessly spiritual guides.

Number 22: Realization

The energy of 22 is the 4 energy that the builder that is put to the service of others, due to that double-two. This is the power of realizing and the ability to put into action the ideals one has in mind. A person is able to turn his ideas into reality. He is a publicist and can implement public works or develop cutting-edge technology. He's got the ability to leadership and determination. His strength is in creating.

Number 33: Teaching

This is the number that is the master of the master of the universe, also known as the one who is the savior. It is the number that represents the master of communication, therefore those with this number are typically souls who have come to earth to assist others to regain their connection to the spiritual realm through using words. The compassionate one that works in the field of human rights and may be an educator. Master 33 refers to person who is unconditionally loved. His strength is communication.

Number 44: Government

In the case of the 44 energy, you can conclude that the power behind this number is that of the regent master. It's about the one who directs the society towards the proper direction. However, it also represents an energy that is deeply linked to the earth, and the master44 is there to aid those who have earth-related issues as well as material problems. He is an ecologist, a regnant and veterinary professional or biologist, who works to safeguard animals and earth as well as or a dietician. The power of matter.

Chapter 16: For better understanding

A quick chart of numerology

Marilyn Monroe

The birth name is Norma Jeane Mortenson Baker

Birth date 01/06/1926

Day: 1

Destiny: 1 + 6 + 9 = 16/7

Life Path 7+8 + 7 +1 = 23/5

Heart's desire: 7 + 11 + 8 + 6 = 32/5

Personality: 9 + 6 + 8 + 4 = 27/9

Maturity: 7 + 5 = 12/3

Day 1:

Hers was the most gorgeous woman in her day.

- Desire to win

- She developed her own production company

She was the top one beauty model

- A strong sense of Self

Destiny 16/7:

- High intelligence

Feeling lonely

- Want to be with your own

Feeling ununderstood

Try to achieve perfection

- Sophisticated

- Attention to details

Troubled Life

Family concerns

- Sexually sexually

Heart's desire 32/5:

She was a free soul

She had many husbands and partners

She suffered from addictions

The energy of both of them made her appear elegant and soft appearance

The power that the 3 gave her the idea of the star, which was

- Curiosity

- The desire to be adventurous

The desire to live your the life

- Intelligence

Personality 9:

She had a very humane side

She contributed a great deal of money to assist children at in various ways

Maturity 3:

She was bound to be a celebrity and express herself in a unique way

Chapter 17: Tips and tricks!

Tips and suggestions for the number one spot

Be aware of the way you tend to rule: be aware of your tendencies to rule, which can be exaggerated to the point of absurdity. You may be the intolerant and bully one. Try to be more considerate of others at times and be more friendly.

Beware of loneliness: as one, you are likely to work by yourself. However, this could lead to a total loneliness which isn't good for anyone. Therefore, you should try to show your independence without separating yourself from the rest of the world.

Intimacy: In a relationship you believe you're the right person, and others make mistakes. You should strive being more open in your relationships and try to be more co-operative and open with your spouse.

Job: Try to work as a freelancer and start your own business.

Tips and tricks for the number 2

Self-confidence: strive to maintain your self-confidence, even if you are the other. You may like to hide in the shadows, letting others take the spotlight however this shouldn't be a reason to cause you to feel that you're not as important or insignificant to other people. Your rules are fundamental as you are the roots of the tree.

Avoid victimhood: It is common to appear to be the victim in the event usually when it comes to family, but you may be this way when you are with acquaintances. Be aware that it isn't always the other's blame in the event of a problem and victimhood can create the impression of an unpleasant person. In the end, it's not beneficial for your health.

Relationships: it is important to find an arrangement that allows you to you can best express two energy levels, however, you should be wary of squeezing yourself into a one relationship. There's more to life than just staying at home with a partner and you may suffer from depression if you stay too much in four walls in the same space each day.

Enhance your capacity to take care of others Try to get an employment in the field of health, where you could be of helping other people.

Tips and tips for the number 3

Take note of your tendencies to glamor: you are likely to focus on objects of material and appearance. Be aware that this may cause you to appear too shallow and others will view you in a way that is not appropriate.

Create a strong relationship Try to find an individual you can cherish, even if it seems like you love being the spotlight of many people. It is possible to do this by making a lot of acquaintances and by obtaining jobs that allow for the presence of the public. However, you must ensure that you find someone with whom you have a genuine relationship.

You must work with a crowd communication skill and need to interact with other people. Look for a job that allows you to showcase your creative or artistic skills.

Tips and suggestions for number 4.

Take a step outside of your mind: You tend to get caught up in your logical thinking. This is why it might be beneficial to think outside of your logic, and without placing yourself in danger obviously!

Create plans: you will be able to succeed in making plans for your career and life. This is what you are good at and your forte. Of course , you don't need to overstate your abilities, as you'll also have to make time for relaxation.

It is impossible to manage everything. Not everything can be into your control. Just keep in mind. Sometimes things must be accepted for what they are.

You should try to balance the hours of work and the time for relaxation: you have a tendency to live a sedentary life! Be aware that relaxation is as essential as being productive. You must be in equilibrium, and you cannot simply pick one.

Tips and suggestions for the number 5

Be aware of the things that could make you dependent There are certain things you must manage, particularly like alcohol, nicotine, and food items, and alcohol. There is a higher chance of developing dependence than others.

Travelling can make you feel great. Make time for it.

Study: Find something that catches your interest. You're curious, and should cultivate this curiosity. You can be a successful researcher if you can find something you enjoy in.

Experience: It is important to be having fun and enjoying life and enjoy yourself, that's what you're supposed do. It is essential to experience life and avoid putting yourself in an atmosphere of shyness or avoidance as you'll have many regrets when you get older. Be sure to remember that everything must be done with a sense of balance.

Tips and tips to number 6

Keep your family close: it is important to spend time with your family members, having meals together, participating in things, taking excursions. This is crucial for you. Be sure to take the time to yourself, your family, as well as your significant other.

Create your family. You could be a fantastic parent if you are able to find the right person to start the family you want to have.

Find a way to assist others Consider putting yourself in a social and humane organization, or to find a job that gives you the chance of helping others.

Teaching: You could be an excellent teacher, but you also have to be an excellent coach.

Avoid being a victim: you are likely to act as the victim and blame the problem to others.

Beware of the need to be always the right side of an argument You are the person who is always looking to be right, and cannot think of making mistakes. This isn't true You can't always be right and you need to learn to be open to the opinions of others since everybody has something to learn from. This is a tendency that can cause you to suffer from problems with your family, acquaintances and your partner.

Offer a shoulder people can lean on. You are perfect to be the person whom people can talk to when they're feeling down. Therefore, you must strive to be available whenever people require them. Be aware that some people may profit from your desire to be helpful, and you need to know how to refuse to help.

Tips and tips for number 7

Make time to study If you study you could become an expert in a particular area and it will leave you feeling satisfied.

Be aware of loneliness. You could become a loner If you try to stay away from it!

Avoid harsh criticism. You could be a bit harsh and make people turn out of your way. Use your criticism to benefit others and at the right circumstances.

Do not feel as if you are doing something wrong. If you feel differently, it's because you're different but there's nothing wrong. Your distinctiveness is the reason you are unique and that's exactly the thing that will help you achieve success.

Choose a spiritual competition to keep your faith from fading away in humanity as well as the world at large.

Tips and tricks for number 8

Be patient: Learn become more patient with your family and friends. Be understanding because nobody is perfect, nor you are, and all of us make mistakes from time to time.

Be cautious with your money Don't lose your chance and keep your business secure and well-organized. Be a good business owner as well as a dealmaker and keep even if you fail to succeed the first time around, as you've got the drive to make it in this field.

Expression of emotion: If for you , it's too difficult to express your emotions to the people you feel strongly about, consulting a therapist might be a good idea. It is important to be able to express your emotions and not keep them inside your head otherwise you'll lose connection with them. This can make your family members, and most of all your children be a bit hurt, as the way you express your feelings of love for them can make them believe they don't really love you even a bit.

Chapter 18: People born

The 1st of October 19, and 28 are born with their birth date as 1. The people born on the 1 are guided by the "Sun". They are the most unique in their approach. They are vivacious people who believe in the power of originality and gain immense power.

This represents confidence and courage. 1 , being the first in this series, makes these people extremely secure and self-sufficient. They are naturally leaders, and they love their freedom. They are ambitious and have an intense drive to succeed.

The people in the top 1 percent are adventurous, innovative and brave. They are able to use new and unknown strategies. They are researchers and innovators and are extremely energetic. They are highly skilled and are the most successful in managing their own company.

People in the top tier are extremely imaginative and have sharp and sharp minds. They possess excellent business acumen and, with the right training , they can manage large companies and organizations. They possess excellent management skills. This, together with their excellent planning skills helps them manage their individuals effectively.

The people listed as 1 have leadership skills and an intense drive to succeed. They are inclined towards personal gain, consisting of materialistic desires, and worldly needs. They are awed by dominating others, and putting their dominant personality at the front. They are both status and appearance aware, and they are opinion makers. They love cleanliness and would like to live a an extravagant lifestyle.

The most notable thing about one people has to do with their dedication, determination and ingenuity that gives them financial and personal success. 1 people their birth date must be free of making their own choices and based on their personal concepts. Any form of limit or restrictions frustrate them.

People with this type of personality tend toward being self-centered. They generally are open to the thoughts of others, but they can be extremely stubborn and obstinate when they are enslaved to their ideas. They may be dominant at times, and in extreme instances, an aggressive bully. They can be extremely criticizing others, and complaining that people don't have their determination However, they must be able to accept their position otherwise, this lack of understanding could cause alienation to their family and friends from them.

These are loyal, committed family members and may show a display of their love for one another. They are also extremely competitive and be jealous in relation to the accomplishments of others, particularly friends or colleagues. They want to always achieve the highest level and achieve success, but even if they can't see this happening or seeing other people move ahead of them, this makes them unhappy.

It is important to avoid lazyness and procrastination. They are easily angry and annoyed and are prone to push for change at moments when things aren't progressing as quickly as they'd like to. They aren't a fan of routines and enjoy a variety of changes in life. They may become bored or even depressed when things don't go according to their expectations. To avoid the pitfalls of this kind it is necessary to take a calculated risk. Sometimes, they can exhibit selfishness and a self-serving mindset. They should try to keep from exaggerating and going too much.

They typically complete their higher education. The ideal job for them could be an inventor or innovator, managing, banking and scientific jobs are suitable for them.

People born on the dates 2,11,20,29 will have their birth s as 2. 2 "Moon" governs 2 people. There is always a great relationship between people who have 1 and 2, since 2 is the half of one. Actually, people who are 2 possess the qualities of 1, however they aren't as determined in showing it since they are ruled over by moon, which is feminine in the natural world.

The people who have this exhibit dualistic natures. The people with the 2 are extremely emotionally and caring. They have a positive personality and look attractive too. They are at ease with their surroundings. But they are also humble, modest and gentle in their own way. Their sensitive nature makes them highly sensitive and vulnerable to hurt.

They're not physically powerful, but they are masters of their intellect. They possess a high-level of sense of. Their intuition lets them discern what people want before they express it. This allows them to gain an understanding of people and their needs and can make them the ideal diplomat.

The second group of people aren't proficient in the beginning of a project. They frequently require motivation and moral support to continue because it's difficult to successfully complete the project by themselves. they are able to continue an undertaking better than begin it on their own. Once they're in a project they're the glue that holds groups in a group.

Although they may not receive all the attention they merit, they are essential in every endeavor. Their skills are best displayed when they work with others rather as opposed to working on their own. They are affectionate and warm and require the same from close family and friends. They would like to be kissed and hugged. It is common for them to get into childhood routines when it comes to giving and receiving affection. People want to feel safe and secure.

People put on too much stress over the smallest thing and are uneasy. Due to the moonlike nature, they can be unstable. They come up with a variety of concepts but rarely stick to one. Some people take advantage of their position due to their tolerance and, eventually, they get injured. They are selfless but they do not always meet selfless people in the real world.

The second group of people are nice in heart. When other people progress, they are happy for them. they do not feel ill-will or be jealous of any person. Serving others and helping them is the basic quality of people who rank second. They are able to say no to anyone with ease.

The second thing to do is maintain their positive outlook and never lose confidence They are much more than they believe. If they aren't confident, they are more susceptible to depression. If they are not balanced They can quickly get stressed and over-stimulated. They can easily fall victim to mood swings, injuries and injuries. These people are dependent, and unsecure with their relationships. Therefore, they are always looking for stability security, love and security in their relationships. They constantly seek to escape the wrath and squabbles.

The most suitable professions for them could include teaching, counseling as well as designing, architecture and even music. They could also work as diplomats, advisors, and healers.

The people born with s 3 12 and 30 are born with their base of 3.This is controlled by the Planet "Jupiter". 3. represents energy, balance, and consciousness.

Three s make them self-confident, ambitious, and highly progressive. People who fall under the numerology 3 are most energetic. They are social creatures They are awed and long to be social. They are confident and positive and have a positive attitude towards everything.

They are happy and carefree, fun with a sense of fun and joyful. They possess a strong imagination and creativity, along with artistic abilities. They possess a stunning personality with an endless energy. Three factors make a person a an effective leader and is a success in society. They are energy hungry. They're friendly social and loving in their nature. They have a lot of charisma. They are extremely enthusiastic. They possess a great ability to create harmony as well as beauty in everything they do, from their attire to how they decorate their homes.

Physically and mentally, three people are extremely strong. They believe in the power of doing things. They are clear in their thought processes and they are awed by people who follow and listen to them. They are practical throughout their lives. The have their individual ideas and ideas.

They are extremely proficient in communication acting, writing, and speaking abilities and a plethora of self-expression. They love to communicate with other people and utilize it as a tool to express themselves. They don't believe in taking things seriously all the time and thus enjoy every second of their lives with enthusiasm and enthusiasm. They are great at love, romance and romance.

These people are religious, and respect for their beliefs, therefore, they value their beliefs. They are adaptable, persevering and dedicated to their work. The pursuit of adventure is a major aspect of their lives. They love to travel, and their destiny provides them with many opportunities in this area.

They are prone to spending a lot and even though they're prudent in their spending habits, there are times when they just want to impress to other people. Even though they're lavish but they never run out of cash. Because of their personalities and other traits, they are able to reach the top of the heap in very little time. However, they must be cautious not to overuse their skills. The problem is that they frequently lack discipline and discipline in their lives.

Beware of becoming an "happy- go-lucky" spendthrift avoids the responsibility and commitment. They should learn to be able to concentrate and be focused. They are often anxious and prone to rapid fluctuations. Be cautious not to spend time and energy on nit-picky things. Make sure your priorities for the long term are in the present.

These are the main factors that contribute to the third person's success. They are naive and critical of other people and enjoy gossip. They don't like it when they should be challenged and challenge them because they like to dictate their own opinions. They should take care that they should not be spending a lot of money and shouldn't be envious of others or abuse their authority.

Chapter 19: A good profession

Them could include teaching, banking or acting. They can be scholars, scientists and even business executives.

People born on the s 4 13, 22, and 31 have their birth s as 4. People born on 4 are affected by the planet "Rahu". They are subject to several ups and downs in their lives. On one day, they're wealthy and the next they'd be struggling to survive and that is how life is. Many unexpected events occur throughout their lives.

This signifies turmoil changes, fortune, change and practicality. In the world, they can either get up to the top or to the lowest. Their decisions are often altered, and in reality the thoughts they have in their heads, even their relatives are unable to comprehend. They can be angry immediately and become normal quickly. Due to their nature , they have many friends, but they need to be vigilant regarding their relationships with friends, since they will be using them to fulfill their own needs, therefore they shouldn't trust anyone in complete faith.

They are hard-working and a meticulous person. They are disciplined, highly principled and accountable. They are very serious about their obligations. The 4th person appears proud and upright, however they're not especially confident. They care about people. They truly love people, their families, friends and can be a great acquaintance themselves. They aren't overly emotional or displaying of their affection. They tend to minimize their feelings. They're always focussed on the fundamentals of their lives. Whether it's work, career or family issues, they focus on the basics and deal with the situation with a mature manner. They are extremely intelligent and have a natural ability to organize.

The 4th person makes good managers. People, in particular friends and family members, are likely to depend on them. They are seen as the core of any project. Certain, their perspective regarding all issues is distinct from the rest of us. They generally expose people to their side that no one else has given much thought to.

But when they think and speak exactly the opposite to others and state their opinions so strongly, they find them to be arrogant, and their friends become adversaries, so they have many hidden enemies. But they are not harmed with openness due to the explosive character of their a strong personality. Their lives are not easy, and even if they think it is a good thing it's likely to take unexpected twists and turns and then bewilder all.

In their hearts, these people are practical, logical as well as considerate and reliable. However , it is difficult to comprehend them. They are always full of energy. Their behavior for all people is always a will I do something for you. They're not spendthrifts nor misers , but their spending is always higher than their income.

Deep in the heart they will always feel alone. Because of their temperamental instability, they become bored with the things they do. If they're in a job, they do not stay for long. Even though they have all the options for a comfortable life and they believe there is something missing. they are often uncompromising and rigid. This type of attitude may hinder their ability to come up with innovative ideas or solutions Therefore, they need to be more flexible.

A lot of them experience anger and feelings of repression. They're not people who are emotionally driven who are able to completely comprehend the emotional world. Because of the many challenges that they face as a result of their lives They should not let their patience go and abandon everything in between. It's their willpower that will propel them to greater high places. Be careful to not overwork themselves and avoiding the opportunity to smell the flowers of life. It is advised to not do too many tasks at one time. They must try to stay from being in the spotlight, avoid gossip, and refrain from criticizing individuals. Finally, they should allocate their time in accordance with their capacities.

The best career options for them would be in accounting, banking as well as law and science related. They are skilled planners, technicians and politicians.

People born on the dates of 5, 14 and 23 are assigned their birth date or birth date as 5. The 5 is governed by "Mercury". It represents wisdom and understanding. Mercury being the god of communication, 5, people are highly communicative and educated. They cherish their freedom. Freedom is the axis that revolves their lives.

Five people in the top 5 like change, travel and adventures. They are extremely curious and long to visit remote locations and meet new people. They excel in a variety of kinds of abilities. They are positive, encouraging positive, happy, and reflect the spirit of. The top five people are highly adaptable and require a sense of enthusiasm. They are able to connect with others and are able to communicate to communicate.

They are able to work with other people in the event that there aren't too many limitations. These people aren't bound by routines. They struggle to be tied to a desk or an office. They often feel stuck and isolated in the absence of variety and changes in their lives. They're so unfocused in nature that they can become bored quickly.

They might be reckless and require discipline and discipline. They have a quick , analytical brain. They might be confident and confident, but they're extremely creative. They are able to make friends and keep their friendships too. They're also sentimental. They are masters at communicating communications, and are equipped with amazing communication skills. They are awe-inspiring and magnetic traits.

Humorousness is an integral an aspect of their character as well. When it comes to money, their fate changes, however, they are financially sound. They are able to manage their expenses. They earn quick profits. Since they enjoy the constant changes that life brings, they don't shy away from taking risks. Their minds are always racing to discover something different. They can learn easily and can adapt to the new environment quickly.

They possess a charming appeal to their appearance that draws everyone's attention, regardless of age young or children. They also display the simplicity and innocence of their character and are trustworthy. Five people have an optimistic outlook on life and do not easily get discouraged. They view everything with a positive outlook and negative thought is not a problem for them. They are extremely strong in their mind and body and do not give up easily. Their character is unchangeable.

They are great leaders, however they do not have the leadership excellence that the top people possess in them. They can handle different tasks at a given point of time. If someone is in a work in partnership with them, they too will benefit. They might not be able to perform physically but they're always on the lookout. Their thoughts are precise, but they also like to force their ideas on other people, which they must be avoiding.

It is essential to guard themselves from ravages of taste. Five people are smart and quick-thinkers, but their thinking processes - just like their general life can be chaotic and scattered. They are prone to falling in and out of relationships frequently, particularly when they are young. They are unstable in their relationships. It is hard for them to remain committed to their relationships, which is why they have numerous relationships to choose from. They encounter difficulties when it comes to the execution of their plans, since they remain aloof when they need discipline and disciplined manners. They lack patience and easily get caught in the tangle of worry and unrest. They are prone to being distracted quickly. Sometimes, they display impulsive behavior. They must remain calm and focused if they wish to succeed.

Careers that are suitable for them could be in the entertainment industry or sales. They can also work in travel. They could be promoted, entrepreneurs, bankers, and investors.

People born on the dates of 6, 15 and 24 are referred to as having their birth date as 6. People born on 6 are ruled by "Venus". They are the most caring of all. They possess compassion as their particular characteristic. They are friendly, compassionate generous, compassionate, and well-balanced in their character.

They are generous and kind in heart and soul. They are never afraid to take on their obligations. They are magnets, charming and awe. They display the stability, loyalty and dedication to their relationships. They enrich their relationships by providing compassion, love and love.

This symbolises affection and love. This makes them very attractive and distinct from others. The 6th person is a kind and compassionate people who have tendencies to prioritize people's needs ahead of their own needs. They are reliable and trustworthy with a respect for honesty and justice. They are creative. Beauty and harmony are top on their priority list.

They possess a lot of artistic talent and an innate appreciation for art and beauty.

Although they are musically talented, however, the artistic talents of the 6 are often neglected or ignored because they tend to give up their time and their pleasure for the benefit of other people.

They are family-oriented and possess an ability to resolve disputes among people to the satisfaction of both parties. They are extremely accountable and will do whatever to settle an debt.They must know that they are respected. They are prone praise and praise. However, criticism however can leave a negative image on their faces.

They will take this to the core. They are willing to sacrifice their own comfort to help and support others. They are generous, caring and understanding. They can be extremely emotional and prone to extremes of emotional sensitivity and sympathy. They need to learn to be more than just the support of a friend. They are often using cosmetics. Deodorant, fragrance after-shave lotion, and other perfumed items are essential for their needs. Men aren't developed, however they have a pleasant persona. They want everything in their homes to be well designed and elegantly decorated. They are awestruck by nature. They are attracted by natural beauty such as forests mountains, seashores or mountains.

They like to dress up and dress up in accessories. They are not extremely wealthy but they do are prone to spending a lot on romance and glamour. They are willing to go to the extreme to satisfy those they love dearly in their lives. They're great hosts. They don't have a lot of anger but they also don't tolerate any kind of opposition. They're very generous in their nature.

They are a party animal and are often referred to as party animals. Basically, they are the main attraction at every celebration. They believe in God often. However , the 6 individuals are extremely emotional. Sometimes, they become so self-sacrificing , they will sacrifice their desires, needs or talents and those they love to please other people. It is important to be cautious when forming relationships with people of opposite sexual partners, since they could be easily sucked into to ride.

They should be extremely prudent with their spending habits; they have a tendency of spending money that is not needed. It is essential to be aware of their diet. They shouldn't try to try to dictate their thoughts on others and should not rely on any person in complete faith. They have to face challenges when it comes to defining their personal identity

Chapter 20: always carrying a load of stress on their shoulders.

These individuals can be excellent musicians, healers, teachers and artists, crafters journalists, actors and more.

People born on the 1st of October 19, and 28 are born with their birth date as 1. The people born on the 1 are guided by the "Sun". They are the most unique in their approach. They are vivacious people who believe in the power of originality and gain immense power.

This represents confidence and courage. 1 , being the first in this series, makes these people extremely secure and self-sufficient. They are naturally leaders, and they love their freedom. They are ambitious and have an intense drive to succeed.

The people in the top 1 percent are adventurous, innovative and brave. They are able to use new and unknown strategies. They are researchers and innovators and are extremely energetic. They are highly skilled and are the most successful in managing their own company.

People in the top tier are extremely imaginative and have sharp and sharp minds. They possess excellent business acumen and, with the right training , they can manage large companies and organizations. They possess excellent management skills. This, together with their excellent planning skills helps them manage their individuals effectively.

The people listed as 1 have leadership skills and an intense drive to succeed. They are inclined towards personal gain, consisting of materialistic desires, and worldly needs. They are awed by dominating others, and putting their dominant personality at the front. They are both status and appearance aware, and they are opinion makers. They love cleanliness and would like to live a an extravagant lifestyle.

The most notable thing about one people has to do with their dedication, determination and ingenuity that gives them financial and personal success. 1 people their birth date must be free of making their own choices and based on their personal concepts. Any form of limit or restrictions frustrate them.

People with this type of personality tend toward being self-centered. They generally are open to the thoughts of others, but they can be extremely stubborn and obstinate when they are enslaved to their ideas. They may be dominant at times, and in extreme instances, an aggressive bully. They can be extremely criticizing others, and complaining that people don't have their determination However, they must be able to accept their position otherwise, this lack of understanding could cause alienation to their family and friends from them.

These are loyal, committed family members and may show a display of their love for one another. They are also extremely competitive and be jealous in relation to the accomplishments of others, particularly friends or colleagues. They want to always achieve the highest level and achieve success, but even if they can't see this happening or seeing other people move ahead of them, this makes them unhappy.

It is important to avoid lazyness and procrastination. They are easily angry and annoyed and are prone to push for change at moments when things aren't progressing as quickly as they'd like to. They aren't a fan of routines and enjoy a variety of changes in life. They may become bored or even depressed when things don't go according to their expectations. To avoid the pitfalls of this kind it is necessary to take a calculated risk. Sometimes, they can exhibit selfishness and a self-serving mindset. They should try to keep from exaggerating and going too much.

They typically complete their higher education. The ideal job for them could be an inventor or innovator, managing, banking and scientific jobs are suitable for them.

People born on the dates 2,11,20,29 will have their birth s as 2. 2 "Moon" governs 2 people. There is always a great relationship between people who have 1 and 2, since 2 is the half of one. Actually, people who are 2 possess the qualities of 1, however they aren't as determined in showing it since they are ruled over by moon, which is feminine in the natural world.

The people who have this exhibit dualistic natures. The people with the 2 are extremely emotionally and caring. They have a positive personality and look attractive too. They are at ease with their surroundings. But they are also humble, modest and gentle in their own way. Their sensitive nature makes them highly sensitive and vulnerable to hurt.

They're not physically powerful, but they are masters of their intellect. They possess a high-level of sense of. Their intuition lets them discern what people want before they express it. This allows them to gain an understanding of people and their needs and can make them the ideal diplomat.

The second group of people aren't proficient in the beginning of a project. They frequently require motivation and moral support to continue because it's difficult to successfully complete the project by themselves. they are able to continue an undertaking better than begin it on their own. Once they're in a project they're the glue that holds groups in a group.

Although they may not receive all the attention they merit, they are essential in every endeavor. Their skills are best displayed when they work with others rather as opposed to working on their own. They are affectionate and warm and require the same from close family and friends.

They would like to be kissed and hugged. It is common for them to get into childhood routines when it comes to giving and receiving affection. People want to feel safe and secure.

People put on too much stress over the smallest thing and are uneasy. Due to the moonlike nature, they can be unstable. They come up with a variety of concepts but rarely stick to one. Some people take advantage of their position due to their tolerance and, eventually, they get injured. They are selfless but they do not always meet selfless people in the real world.

The second group of people are nice in heart. When other people progress, they are happy for them. they do not feel ill-will or be jealous of any person. Serving others and helping them is the basic quality of people who rank second. They are able to say no to anyone with ease.

The second thing to do is maintain their positive outlook and never lose confidence They are much more than they believe. If they aren't confident, they are more susceptible to depression. If they are not balanced They can quickly get stressed and over-stimulated. They can easily fall victim to mood swings, injuries and injuries. These people are dependent, and unsecure with their relationships. Therefore, they are always looking for stability security, love and security in their relationships. They constantly seek to escape the wrath and squabbles.

The most suitable professions for them could include teaching, counseling as well as designing, architecture and even music. They could also work as diplomats, advisors, and healers.

The people born with s 3 12 and 30 are born with their base of 3.This is controlled by the Planet "Jupiter". 3. represents energy, balance, and consciousness.

Three s make them self-confident, ambitious, and highly progressive. People who fall under the numerology 3 are most energetic. They are social creatures They are awed and long to be social. They are confident and positive and have a positive attitude towards everything.

They are happy and carefree, fun with a sense of fun and joyful. They possess a strong imagination and creativity, along with artistic abilities. They possess a stunning personality with an endless energy. Three factors make a person a an effective leader and is a success in society. They are energy hungry. They're friendly social and loving in their nature. They have a lot of charisma. They are extremely enthusiastic. They possess a great ability to create harmony as well as beauty in everything they do, from their attire to how they decorate their homes.

Chapter 21: Physically and mentally

people are extremely strong. They believe in the power of doing things. They are clear in their thought processes and they are awed by people who follow and listen to them. They are practical throughout their lives. The have their individual ideas and ideas.

They are extremely proficient in communication acting, writing, and speaking abilities and a plethora of self-expression. They love to communicate with other people and utilize it as a tool to express themselves. They don't believe in taking things seriously all the time and thus enjoy every second of their lives with enthusiasm and enthusiasm. They are great at love, romance and romance.

These people are religious, and respect for their beliefs, therefore, they value their beliefs. They are adaptable, persevering and dedicated to their work. The pursuit of adventure is a major aspect of their lives.

They love to travel, and their destiny provides them with many opportunities in this area.

They are prone to spending a lot and even though they're prudent in their spending habits, there are times when they just want to impress to other people. Even though they're lavish but they never run out of cash. Because of their personalities and other traits, they are able to reach the top of the heap in very little time. However, they must be cautious not to overuse their skills. The problem is that they frequently lack discipline and discipline in their lives.

Beware of becoming an "happy- go-lucky" spendthrift avoids the responsibility and commitment. They should learn to be able to concentrate and be focused. They are often anxious and prone to rapid fluctuations. Be cautious not to spend time and energy on nit-picky things. Make sure your priorities for the long term are in the present.

These are the main factors that contribute to the third person's success. They are naive and critical of other people and enjoy gossip. They don't like it when they should be challenged and challenge them because they like to dictate their own opinions. They should take care that they should not be spending a lot of money and shouldn't be envious of others or abuse their authority.

A good profession for them could include teaching, banking or acting. They can be scholars, scientists and even business executives.

People born on the s 4 13, 22, and 31 have their birth s as 4. People born on 4 are affected by the planet "Rahu". They are subject to several ups and downs in their lives. On one day, they're wealthy and the next they'd be struggling to survive and that is how life is. Many unexpected events occur throughout their lives.

This signifies turmoil changes, fortune, change and practicality. In the world, they can either get up to the top or to the lowest. Their decisions are often altered, and in reality the thoughts they have in their heads, even their relatives are unable to comprehend. They can be angry immediately and become normal quickly. Due to their nature , they have many friends, but they need to be vigilant regarding their relationships with friends, since they will be using them to fulfill their own needs, therefore they shouldn't trust anyone in complete faith.

They are hard-working and a meticulous person. They are disciplined, highly principled and accountable. They are very serious about their obligations. The 4th person appears proud and upright, however they're not especially confident. They care about people. They truly love people, their families, friends and can be a great acquaintance themselves. They aren't overly emotional or displaying of their affection. They tend to minimize their feelings. They're always focussed on the fundamentals of their lives. Whether it's work, career or family issues, they focus on the basics and deal with the situation with a mature manner. They are extremely intelligent and have a natural ability to organize.

The 4th person makes good managers. People, in particular friends and family members, are likely to depend on them. They are seen as the core of any project. Certain, their perspective regarding all issues is distinct from the rest of us. They generally expose people to their side that no one else has given much thought to.

But when they think and speak exactly the opposite to others and state their opinions so strongly, they find them to be arrogant, and their friends become adversaries, so they have many hidden enemies. But they are not harmed with openness due to the explosive character of their a strong personality. Their lives are not easy, and even if they think it is a good thing it's likely to take unexpected twists and turns and then bewilder all.

In their hearts, these people are practical, logical as well as considerate and reliable. However , it is difficult to comprehend them. They are always full of energy. Their behavior for all people is always a will I do something for you. They're not spendthrifts nor misers , but their spending is always higher than their income.

Deep in the heart they will always feel alone. Because of their temperamental instability, they become bored with the things they do. If they're in a job, they do not stay for long. Even though they have all the options for a comfortable life and they believe there is something missing. they are often uncompromising and rigid. This type of attitude may hinder their ability to come up with innovative ideas or solutions Therefore, they need to be more flexible.

A lot of them experience anger and feelings of repression. They're not people who are emotionally driven who are able to completely comprehend the emotional world. Because of the many challenges that they face as a result of their lives They should not let their patience go and abandon everything in between. It's their willpower that will propel them to greater high places. Be careful to not overwork themselves and avoiding the opportunity to smell the flowers of life. It is advised to not do too many tasks at one time. They must try to stay from being in the spotlight, avoid gossip, and refrain from criticizing individuals. Finally, they should allocate their time in accordance with their capacities.

The best career options for them would be in accounting, banking as well as law and science related. They are skilled planners, technicians and politicians.

People born on the dates of 5, 14 and 23 are assigned their birth date or birth date as 5. The 5 is governed by "Mercury". It represents wisdom and understanding. Mercury being the god of communication, 5, people are highly communicative and educated. They cherish their freedom. Freedom is the axis that revolves their lives.

Five people in the top 5 like change, travel and adventures. They are extremely curious and long to visit remote locations and meet new people. They excel in a variety of kinds of abilities. They are positive, encouraging positive, happy, and reflect the spirit of. The top five people are highly adaptable and require a sense of enthusiasm. They are able to connect with others and are able to communicate to communicate.

They are able to work with other people in the event that there aren't too many limitations. These people aren't bound by routines. They struggle to be tied to a desk or an office. They often feel stuck and isolated in the absence of variety and changes in their lives. They're so unfocused in nature that they can become bored quickly.

They might be reckless and require discipline and discipline. They have a quick , analytical brain. They might be confident and confident, but they're extremely creative. They are able to make friends and keep their friendships too. They're also sentimental. They are masters at communicating communications, and are equipped with amazing communication skills. They are awe-inspiring and magnetic traits.

Humorousness is an integral an aspect of their character as well. When it comes to money, their fate changes, however, they are financially sound. They are able to manage their expenses. They earn quick profits. Since they enjoy the constant changes that life brings, they don't shy away from taking risks. Their minds are always racing to discover something different. They can learn easily and can adapt to the new environment quickly.

They possess a charming appeal to their appearance that draws everyone's attention, regardless of age young or children. They also display the simplicity and innocence of their character and are trustworthy. Five people have an optimistic outlook on life and do not easily get discouraged. They view everything with a positive outlook and negative thought is not a problem for them. They are extremely strong in their mind and body and do not give up easily. Their character is unchangeable.

They are great leaders, however they do not have the leadership excellence that the top people possess in them. They can handle different tasks at a given point of time. If someone is in a work in partnership with them, they too will benefit. They might not be able to perform physically but they're always on the lookout. Their thoughts are precise, but they also like to force their ideas on other people, which they must be avoiding.

It is essential to guard themselves from ravages of taste. Five people are smart and quick-thinkers, but their thinking processes - just like their general life can be chaotic and scattered. They are prone to falling in and out of relationships frequently, particularly when they are young. They are unstable in their relationships. It is hard for them to remain committed to their relationships, which is why they have numerous relationships to choose from. They encounter difficulties when it comes to the execution of their plans, since they remain aloof when they need discipline and disciplined manners. They lack patience and easily get caught in the tangle of worry and unrest. They are prone to being distracted quickly. Sometimes, they display impulsive behavior. They must remain calm and focused if they wish to succeed.

Careers that are suitable for them could be in the entertainment industry or sales. They can also work in travel. They could be promoted, entrepreneurs, bankers, and investors.

People born on the dates of 6, 15 and 24 are referred to as having their birth date as 6. People born on 6 are ruled by "Venus". They are the most caring of all. They possess compassion as their particular characteristic. They are friendly, compassionate generous, compassionate, and well-balanced in their character.

They are generous and kind in heart and soul. They are never afraid to take on their obligations. They are magnets, charming and awe. They display the stability, loyalty and dedication to their relationships. They enrich their relationships by providing compassion, love and love.

This symbolises affection and love. This makes them very attractive and distinct from others. The 6th person is a kind and compassionate people who have tendencies to prioritize people's needs ahead of their own needs. They are reliable and trustworthy with a respect for honesty and justice. They are creative. Beauty and harmony are top on their priority list.

They possess a lot of artistic talent and an innate appreciation for art and beauty. Although they are musically talented, however, the artistic talents of the 6 are often neglected or ignored because they tend to give up their time and their pleasure for the benefit of other people.

They are family-oriented and possess an ability to resolve disputes among people to the satisfaction of both parties. They are extremely accountable and will do whatever to settle an debt.They must know that they are respected. They are prone praise and praise. However, criticism however can leave a negative image on their faces.

They will take this to the core. They are willing to sacrifice their own comfort to help and support others. They are generous, caring and understanding. They can be extremely emotional and prone to extremes of emotional sensitivity and sympathy. They need to learn to be more than just the support of a friend. They are often using cosmetics. Deodorant, fragrance after-shave lotion, and other perfumed items are essential for their needs. Men aren't developed, however they have a pleasant persona. They want everything in their homes to be well designed and elegantly decorated. They are awestruck by nature. They are attracted by natural beauty such as forests mountains, seashores or mountains.

They like to dress up and dress up in accessories. They are not extremely wealthy but they do are prone to spending a lot on romance and glamour. They are willing to go to the extreme to satisfy those they love dearly in their lives. They're great hosts. They don't have a lot of anger but they also don't tolerate any kind of opposition. They're very generous in their nature.

They are a party animal and are often referred to as party animals. Basically, they are the main attraction at every celebration. They believe in God often. However , the 6 individuals are extremely emotional. Sometimes, they become so self-sacrificing , they will sacrifice their desires, needs or talents and those they love to please other people. It is important to be cautious when forming relationships with people of opposite sexual partners, since they could be easily sucked into to ride.

They should be extremely prudent with their spending habits; they have a tendency of spending money that is not needed. It is essential to be aware of their diet. They shouldn't try to try to dictate their thoughts on others and should not rely on any person in complete faith. They have to face challenges when it comes to defining their personal identity and are always carrying a load of stress on their shoulders.

These individuals can be excellent musicians, healers, teachers and artists, crafters journalists, actors and more.

Chapter 22: THE SCIENCE OF NUMBERS OR ARITHMOLOGY

"One could also show that modern mathematics represents, so to speak, only the bark of Pythagorean mathematics, its purely 'exoteric' side; the ancient idea of numbers has even become absolutely unintelligible to moderns, because, there too, the superior part of science, that which gave it, along with the traditional character, a properly intellectual value, has totally disappeared." Rene Guenon, The Crisis of the Modern World

"In arithmetic, 1,2,3,4 are compound values of 1x1, 2x1, 3x1, 4x1. But the numbers 1,2,3,4, are abstract points or lines, triangles or squares; they are androgynous or sexual, procreative or progeny, they are active or passive, they are natural elements, life or death, principles, they are not quantities, but the qualities of everything in the world." R.A. Schwaller de Lubicz The Egyptian miracle

The study of numbers is called the Science of Unity, because by studying it, we can see that everything is derived from Unity and all is a return to it in the form of the diversity. This diversity is akin to the sensual world and the world that was created by the infinite universe of Ideas in the Platonic term.

The One, also known as known as the "Upper", divides, and its divisor that is"the "Lower", increases in size and reduces the percentage of Unity. These parts of Unity are the same for all things that happen in our world.

It is the spatially and temporally instabil Origin The Source that is inaccessible to rational thought, the ultimate reality. The Source is polarized according to its own will, and later manifests as a spiritual substance, which is portrayed as the energy from which the universe is constructed. The duality is born and transforms into Trinity an entirely new and creative unity, from which the universe expands in all its facets by a constant oscillation or alternation of different polarities.

The same way the basic unity of a person splitting sexually manifests in the number Two. Sexuality is in reality only the manifestation for the quantity Two. It is recognized this number represents a thing that has more than a quantifiable nature, but also a purpose, since it is only in relation.

In arithmetic we are only interested in the amount represented by numbers: When the symbol "4" uses, it signifies "four units added together". In geometry, the values are merely ratios. For instance, the term Pi is difficult to comprehend as an arithmetic value that claims to be an unchanging quantity. It is, in essence, the proportion between the circle's circumference along with its radius, with the dimensions of the former being irrelevant. Pi is therefore the purpose of the circle, and the number of the circle being of a strictly qualitative nature. From the number it has a geometrical shape which means that, in its concrete aspect it's a lot more purposeful or a ratio than it is a number.

This is apparent in the golden ratio. music harmony... In harmony with music there are three pillars of pure and perfect harmony that are the fifth: 2/3 The fourth: 3/4, and the third: 4/5.

Let us go back to the divine and creative Trinity model and the source of all things, as well as preside over everything. The truth is that Trinity is at the root of everything can be evident in these examples The surface, which is the first known form that must possess at least three sides to exist; three primary colors, red, blue, and yellow, are the basis for all other colors; and the life of the animal is dependent on the male, female and offspring, etc.

Furthermore it is true that the Trinity is actually the root of everything. Everything is fundamentally threefold in its structure For instance, man is a person with an body as well as a soul and spirit. The ancients represented these three Principles of all things , namely Sulfur, Mercury and Salt. Each principle is comprised of one of four elements: Fire and Air in Sulfur as well as Air and Fire in Mercury, Air and Water within Mercury as well as Water in Salt, and Water Earth and Earth in Salt. So seven qualitative factors within that make up that is the Three Principles containing the Four Elements. It is important to note that the entire octave of the scale is comprised of seven notes that are pure and light is broken through the prism (triangle) into seven distinct shades.

In actual fact there are seven distinct elements in each phenomenon, and, from these seven elements Harmony is formed. Harmony is the result of the Trinity and is influenced through the four Elements In the sense that it is an effect of the sevenfold manifestations of The three Principles as well as the Four Elements.

Let us not forget this. The Absolute Unity does not create it, but rather divides or splits as it is eternal and invariable. The manifest reality is the split Unity that is it is the Unity that is contemplating it. The One is not able to reproduce, since it is. Procreation is the result of the third dimension. Therefore, all potentialities of the Universe are found in what Pythagoreans described as Tetraktys $1+2+3+4 = 10$.

I

I I

I I I

I I I I

The combination of the numbers that represent the Unique and the polarization of the procreation, and the first form of procreation (the four) creates God the Divine decade. The numbers are arranged through a triangle, which is the first surface that is possible, meaning that all manifestations occur by the Trinity and is embodied by each of the Four Elements [11 (the three levels within the triangle) to return to the basic Unity because 10 = 1 + 0 = 1.

It is important to remember that nine parts of Tetraktys are organized around one central element, which is the Divine and unintelligible Unit.

Tetraktys Tetraktys represents the metaphysical triangle that is inaccessible to logic. It can be through Trinity which this Universe manifests itself. Therefore by replacing the central , unintelligible Unity by three units that represent the creative basis which is the Ternary We get the Pentactys or to say, the realized Tetraktys.

|

| |

| | |

| | | |

| | | | |

In this case, the original inventive Trinity is enclosed by twelve units. These are the twelve locations of the World which are depicted in the twelve zodiac signs. These twelve units make up the triangle. If we look at them and then count the number of units we can find five units for the base, and three and four for the sides.

It is, therefore, in reality a 3-4-5 triangular that is it is the Sacred Triangle of the ancient Egyptians. In the words of Plutarch: "It seems probable that the Egyptians considered this right-angled triangle to be the most beautiful of all triangles, and that it was to this figure that they compared the nature of the universe." The 3-4-5 triangle formed the basis for the old science of proportions utilized by the builders of the past.

B

A

A I B

A I I B

c c c c c

The twelve units also comprise those of the 12 scale notes, which include the five altered notes i.e. that the twelve notes on the scale of the chromatic, or those of the twelve sixths on the Pythagorean scale. In music, using the sound of 100Hz for the primary note. Note that the note of the octave starts located at 200, with the fifth is at 300 and the next one at 400, three at the 500th. The fifth, and the third make up what is known as the "perfect major chord", according to the ratio 3-4.

If you look at it qualitatively numbers offer a wonderful harmony that runs the entire universe. To be aware of numbers is to understand the fundamental order of Creation It is to understand our purpose for existence and to know our future.

*****

To back up our arguments To support our argument, here's a brief review on the Pythagorean doctrine that was passed on to us by the ancient writers. To remind us, Pythagoras, like many of his illiterate compatriots was educated by the gods of Egypt.

"In his Successions of the Philosophers, Alexander states that he made this other discovery in Pythagorean Memoirs: the monad is the principle of all things; produced by the monad, the indefinite dyad exists as a material substratum for the monad, which is the cause; it is the monad and the indefinite dyad that generate the numbers, then the numbers that generate the points, then the points that generate the lines. These in turn produce the plane figures, which produce the three-dimensional figures, which produce the sensible bodies whose elements are precisely four: fire, water, earth and air, which change and transform themselves entirely into one another; and it is they who give rise to an animated, intelligent and spherical world." Diogenes Laerce, Lives.

"For Pythagoras of Samos, the son of Mnesarchos one of the first person to utilize the term philosophy, the fundamentals include, on one hand, numbers and their connections (which were also referred to as harmony) and on the other hand the elements that comprise both and he called them geometrical. Later , he distinguished monads as well as the indefinite dyad as fundamentals. According to the philosopher the first of these concepts is the one that corresponds to the efficient and formal cause i.e. God's Intellect. The second is the passive and physical cause, i.e. the world visible. However, on contrary He believes that the essence of this number comes from decade. Actually the Greeks as well as all barbarian nations, count to ten before the count begins with the same number. According to him the power of 10 is in the numbers 4 and the Tetrad. This is why when, starting from the unit and adding the four numbers in the beginning to get the number 10. Furthermore when we go over the tetrad, then we also surpass the number 10, or as a result 1 + 2+ 3 times 4 equals 10. This means that the number, as per it, will be contained in the 10 . It is also as per the calculation, is contained in the number 4.

It was precisely because of this that the Pythagoreans made an oath about the Tetrad, which was to they the highest sacred of things:

He was the one who revealed to us our heads

Tetractys, the root and source

Inexhaustible nature

In addition, according to Pythagoras the soul is composed of a tetrad comprising intellect, science, belief and feeling, from which are all science and art and our own quality of a reasonable being. Aetius, Opinions.

"It it is for the descendants of Pythagoras to inquire what was the view of the Master on this issue as he has never written anything. The person who will be the best to provide us with the information is, in my opinion, Philolaos of Taranto. He begins by writing in a somewhat mysterious manner, in several volumes, the meaning of the world and the significance of each one of them. Then after that, before moving on to the study of the essence in the mind, he dives into a fascinating discussion about the notions of weights, measures and measurements in the fields of music, geometry, and arithmetic. He demonstrates that the entire universe is a result of these concepts. (...)

Let's return to Philolaos who, after we've departed and who in the third volume of his books titled Treatise on Rhythms and Metres speaks of the soul this way"The soul is able to enter the body through numbers and thanks to eternal and inseparable harmony'. He adds: The soul is a lover of the body since it grants the soul access to the senses. After death, it is separated from them from their bodies the soul is able to live an eternal life within the world. Claudian Mamert, On the Soul.

"According to Philolaos, number is the all-powerful, self-generated bond that eternally unites the objects of the world." Jamblicus, Commentary on the Arithmetical Introduction of Nicomachus.

"And in fact, every knowable being has a number: without it, nothing can be conceived, nor known." Philolaos quoted in Stobaeus, Choice of Texts.

"The study of the effect and the core of the number should be done in conjunction with the power of the decade. In fact, the power of numbers is immense infinite, perfect, universal, the basis and guide for the celestial and divine life as well as the human experience and in which it is the strength of the year is a part (missing words included). Without it all things would be inaccessible and a mystery.

The nature of numbers is to every human being a cognizant, instructing and guiding about all things that subject to confusion or ignorance. In fact there is nothing that exist would be apparent to anyone, either by itself, nor in relation to any other thing without the quantity and essence of numbers. It is in fact numbers, by giving all things the same quality to the soul via perception, makes them recognizable and comparable to each other in accordance with what the character of the Gnome is because it is the number that gives them a corporeal appearance and differentiates interactions between things as both unlimited and limited. We can see the nature of number as well as its power of action not just in the realm of divine and demonic as well as in every human action and wordsin all areas and in all the activities of art and in the realm of music." Philolaos quoted in Stobaeus in his the Choice of Texts.

"The early philosophers had right in stating that it is essential to be aware of the measurements that comprise the kairos (the seven) because it is the basis of the philosophy. Let us employ it to begin the process of explaining the world. If we ensure that we don't slack off our focus, we'll be able do so without the infamous Delphic principle or principles from Strabo, Hestiaios, Archytas, Aristotle and all the writers of maxims of the same type.

Athenaeus the Mechanist, Poliorcetics of the Greeks.

II. THE MEANING OF NUMBERS

A. According to the modern numerology

1. The ability to assert yourself, mastery, will power, energy, dominance above others leadership, independence, inspira and egocentricity.

2. Association, collaboration, union, listening, mediation, diplomacy, receptivity, intuition, emotionality, sentimentality.

3. Expression creativity and communication. Exuberance brilliance, social ease and intellectual vivacity extrovert, luck the lightness.

4. Construction, realization of concrete and order. Method persistence, organization strength, stability, sense of effort and detail and resistance.

5. Transformation, mobility, change in impulsiveness, flexibility, openness, a sense of freedom and independence, a desire for adventure and travel, growth, innovation.

6. Harmony, aesthetics refined and conciliation serving, family sense and responsibility, scruples are all essential to being useful.

7. Inner life, reflection introspection, analysis, a critical sense, aptitude for study and innovation intelligence, intellectual depth, a taste for study, searching for the truth, subtlety, wisdom.

8. The spirit of entrepreneurship, fighting spirit determination, irreducibility desire for competitiveness, ambition, the seeking strength, materialism, extremism "all or nothing".

9. Self-forgiveness, dedication, altruism as well as dreaming and sensitivity. It is a the sense of sacrifice, intuition vast and

universal visions seeking the ultimate transcendence or the other.

Note In the words of Hades, "0, not being a definite number, oscillates between nothingness and totality, between negation and affirmation; it is like a granary whose abundance and quality depend on the numbers associated with it. It has plasticity and magnetism, mystery and seduction. In general, when found in a numerological result, it signifies hidden gifts and powers that can be awakened, for good or for evil."

Chapter 23: B. According to Sepharial (1920)

1. This number corresponds to Logos The active and positive principle. It refers to assertion, self-assertion and self-assertion. It also refers to positivism, self-asse isolation, egocentrism and self-confidence. dignity and strength. In the sense of religion it refers to the Lord. The philosophical meaning is it refers to the integration and the fundamental unity of everything. In the sense of material it is individualism.

In simple terms In short: Individuality and possibly self-confidence, egocentricity, affirmation and distinction.

2. Antithesis is the number, also of confirmation and witness. It is a symbol of the duality inherent in the nature of life in the world of God as well as Nature, Spirit and Matter and their interrelation. It is a symbol of agreement but also separation and that is, the principle of alternation between subject and object, reflection.

Because it brings together opposing terms or concepts it refers to production, fructification, or combination. It is essentially, the implicit and the explicit.

In short The relationship, the emotional attraction, psychic attraction and antipathy. doubt and uncertainty.

3. The trinity of existence Intelligence, substance, and substance the ternary of force consciousness and matter. Creation preservation, resolution and creation. There are three dimensions. The three postulates are The thinker, thinking and the object. The duality is projected into consciousness through time and space, resulting in an enigma of state like past, present and the future as well as the expansion of self and self-expression, will permeation.

In short: The ability to think as well as wealth and success rise.

4. The reality of the universe and its realization. The universe of matter. The

cube, or the square. The physical laws of logic; reasoning. Appearance, physiognomy, science. The process of perception that creates cognition and experience, as well as the information. Segmentation, cross classification, order. The swastika, or the scroll of law and the succession list of. Discernment, discretion, relativity.

In simple terms the simplest terms: realization, ownership, possession position, credit, the importance.

5. This number is a sign of the expansion. Inclusion, understanding, judgment. Increase, fertility, propagation. Justice, gain, harvest. Reproduction parental responsibility, reward and punishment. Multiplication.

In short In short: Ethics mobility, travel and commerce. Utility, utility.

6. The degree of collaboration. The union and the intertwining connection. Counterpoint, reciprocal action. Interaction

between both the spiritual and physical as well as the mental and physical Psychology, psychism communion, divination with compassion. Telepathy, psychometry. Conversion. Concord, harmony, peace, satisfaction. Goodness, beauty. Restitution. Reconciliation between sexes. Concubinage.

In short: Cooperation, marriage, reciprocity, sympathy, art, music, dance.

7. The amount of completion. Space and time. Duration, distance. Ageing, decay, or endurance Stability, immortality, and stability. The seven age groups and 7 days of week and so on. 7 seals: fundamentals in humankind notepads and hues. The ternary's alliance and the qualterary perfection of man Adam Kadmon; the cycle of evolution; wisdom; perfection, balance, rest.

In short the simplest terms: Balance, contracts treaties, agreements, harmony or discord.

8. Dissolution is the number that occurs when you dissolve. It is a reference to an underlying law that governs cyclical development as well as the point of breaking the line between the natural and spiritual. Reaction, revolution, fracture, rupture, disintegration, segregation, decomposition, anarchism. Injury, separation, divorce. Inspiration, impulse, genius, invention. Deviation, eccentricity, rebellion, aberration, madness.

In short: Reconstruction, negation, dissolution, loss, extinction, evolution.

9. The rate of regeneration. The birth of a new life. Spirituality, expansion of our senses. Premonition remote travel. Telesthesia, dreams, clairvoyance, clairaudience. Pulsation, reforms, nebulosity and rhythm; overcoming, publication shooting predictions, revelations thoughts in waves, dark, appearance, fog and mystery. Exile, mystery.

In short: Penetration, finesse, energy, zeal, detachment.

C. According to John Heydon (1662)

Born on the 10th of September 1629. John Heydon was a Neoplatonist philosopher who was occultist, Rosicrucian Astrologer, astrologer and English lawyer. He was a person whom Sepharial and other esotericists from the 19th century believed as an authoritative source. He released"The Holy Guide," a work "The Holy Guide" in which he provided an esoteric explanation of the numbers. Here's an excerpt from the chapter in question:

"Let no man doubt that all things can be known by Numbers and Letters, for this is what the Pythagorean philosophers as well as the Rosicrucians certified; in numbers reside certain hidden secrets, discovered by few; the Almighty created all things by Number, Measure and Weight, and from this follows the truth of Names and Letters, which were not established at random but according to certain rules unknown to us."

The One: "The One is designated as a number for Concord, Piety, Friendship and Friendship, and is so unified that it is in no way separated into separate parts. One can be described as the universal measurement that is the source and the origin of all numbers, and containing every number in itself, as the starting point of all number, which is the same as it and indestructible When multiplied, it does not produce anything other that itself. It can be described, like I mentioned before indivisible; it is apparent however that when divided , it is not diminished to a smaller size, but instead multiplied into Units. However, the Units are not more or less in comparison to the entire Unity since the component is always smaller than the entire and it is apparent to me that Unity is not divided into pieces however, it is multiplied into multiple parts.

The 1 is referred to as singular, because beyond it there is nothing. However, having no morgue, and without coupling, it directs its own heat towards itself. It is also the source and the final point of all things and all that exists are aspired to the One, since all things originate from the One. Therefore, it is essential that everything join to the one. Since all things are striving to be returned towards the one from whom they came and return to the One, it is essential that they leave the throngs.

Thus, the One represents the Almighty God who is infinite and uncountable and who made all things from Himself, and encapsulating the entire universe in Him; there is only one God that is one Sun and one Phoenix all over the world and one King among bees, and one leader among the flocks and herds because many animals revere the Unity of the One. In the human body, there is a single organ that is the one that leads all others in the heart; there is one element that is able to overcome and piercing all things and everything else, fire. The one thing that God created God is the source of all wonder, occurring everywhere on earth as well as at the top of the universe, within the vegetable, animal and mineral kingdoms. They are all over the world, but known only to very few, not even by its real name, but hidden under Riddles and symbols, and without which neither natural nor Alchemy Magic is able to reach their full or complete conclusion. Through one person, Adam is the beginning of all people and through him, are mortalized; and via Jesus Christ alone are regenerated.

One Lord One God, one Baptism, one faith one Father for everyone, one mediator between God and the human race One Almighty Creator who is greater than all, close to everyone and within the hearts of all people One Jesus Christ, one Lord Jesus Christ, one Holy Spirit One divinity, and the source of all virtues and powers. In the world of intellectuals there is a super-intelligent and the first Creature of God, the fountain of Life, the soul of the universe; and in the realm of the physical world, we have a person as well as an instrument for all the virtues both natural and supernatural. This is the Philosopher's stone. In the world of the lesser it is the heart that is the first to live and dies that organ is called the heart. In the realm of hell, there is a prince of Rebellion among those of the Angels in addition to Darkness This can be described as Lucifer."

The two " The Pythagoreans identified this number as. They referred to the 1 form, which defines and assigns a particular form and property to all things it affects and affects, and the second matter as it is indeterminate and the source of divisibility and size, which is the nature of corporeal matter. Indeterminate, unformed and unlimited, this is the nature of matter until a particular shape imparts its influence to the matter. It is known as Rea due to its fluid nature as well as conflict, fate, and death because they are the results of the connection of the masses with the corporeal. The three elements of movement, generation, and division are the apparent characteristics of human bodies. They also declare that they endure and carry any burdens or changes that the active forms force upon it. It is evident that the Pythagoreans knew the nature of matter by the number 2 which is an extremely relevant symbol of division, which is a prominent property of matter.

The number 2 is known as"The number that represents Science, Memory, and Light and Light, as well as it is the number for Man which is the number of the world below; it is also known as"the number for Charity" as well as of love for each other, of marriage, and of the society. It is also known as Generation and Juno which is the number associated with the sexes and marriage, because there are two genders. 2 is referred to as the middle, or the separation between evil and good and the beginning of the division of mass and destruction. 2. is also the number that causes discord as well as misfortune, confusion and impurity, a bad number. The number 2 is an impurity number, it's unlucky in Invocations and Conjurations of Souls or Spirits of the deceased.

Pythagoras believed the unity concept to be God as well as good intellect and that duality is a sin and poor intelligence, which implies the existence of a material mass; therefore the Pythagoreans claimed that 2 is not a number, but a particular confusion of units. Eusebius claimed they were Pythagoreans named Unity Apollo two conflict, and the temerity.

The number 2 it is believed that when engraved in copper it will attract a Genie who will get the love of a woman. Sometimes it's engraved in Lapis Lazulus or it is in Virgin Wax, the names of the woman and man are written on a parchment that is blank.

Additionally, 2 Testaments, 2 Commandments of Love, 2 dignities of the first 2 humans were the first and 2 types of Spirits both good and bad two Intellectual Creatures that are The Angel and Soul. 2 Solstices, 2 Luminaries, 2 Equinoxes, two elements that produce a soul, specifically Earth and Water There are two rulers of demons in the underworld, specifically Leviathan and Beemoth, as well as two things that the condemned face according to Christ that is, crying and gnashing of teeth.

2. The 2 symbol is believed to represent a lost thing It also helps to determine if an individual will be rich or not."

The Three " The Pythagoreans described it as Triton and Ternary. The theory believed that plants, animals and minerals, as well as in general , all organisms contain three chemical elements within them: Salt, Sulfur and Mercury. The number 3 is a sacred number, one of perfection, a powerful number. There are 3 aspects to God as well as three theological virtues. Hence this number is the one that governs rituals of religious significance, and through its solemnity, sacrifices and prayers can be repeated 3 times. the Pythagoreans employed it for purifications and sanctifications, and it's very appropriate for the signing of contracts and commitments.

The 3 is the three dimensions: Length, Width and Depth. Both corporeal and spiritual things are comprised of three things, which are the beginning, middle and the ending and the entire length of time is broken down into 3parts: both the present, and the future. Every dimension is broken down into three parts things: the line, surface, and the volume. There are three types of souls: the vegetative, sensory as well as the cognitive. 3. The 3rd is dedicated to Ideal forms and the number 2 is dedicated to matter created and the unity of God The Creator.

There are 3 hierarchies for Angelic Spirits, 3 capacities of the intelligent creatures memory, reason, and will. There are three order of blessed people, which are Martyrs of the Confessors, Martyrs of the Innocent and there are 3 Quaternaries of the zodiacal signs, which are ones that remain fixed or mutable, and cardinal. There are also three kinds of Houses: three types: Angular, Succedent, and Cadent. There are three decans for each sign, and 3 lords of each triplicity. There are three fortunes in the planets, three graces with the goddesses three ladies of destiny within the infernal realms Three Judges, three Furies, three Heads of Cerberus.

I. INTRODUCTION TO THE SCIENCE OF NUMBERS OR ARITHMOLOGY

"One could also show that modern mathematics represents, so to speak, only the bark of Pythagorean mathematics, its purely 'exoteric' side; the ancient idea of numbers has even become absolutely unintelligible to moderns, because, there too, the superior part of science, that which gave it, along with the traditional character, a properly intellectual value, has totally disappeared." Rene Guenon, The Crisis of the Modern World

"In arithmetic, 1,2,3,4 are compound values of 1x1, 2x1, 3x1, 4x1. But the numbers 1,2,3,4, are abstract points or lines, triangles or squares; they are androgynous or sexual, procreative or progeny, they are active or passive, they are natural elements, life or death, principles, they are not quantities, but the qualities of everything in the world." R.A. Schwaller de Lubicz The Egyptian miracle

The study of numbers is called the Science of Unity, because by studying it, we can see that everything is derived from Unity and all is a return to it in the form of the diversity. This diversity is akin to the sensual world and the world that was created by the infinite universe of Ideas in the Platonic term.

The One, also known as known as the "Upper", divides, and its divisor that is"the "Lower", increases in size and reduces the percentage of Unity. These parts of Unity are the same for all things that happen in our world.

It is the spatially and temporally instabil Origin The Source that is inaccessible to rational thought, the ultimate reality. The Source is polarized according to its own will, and later manifests as a spiritual substance, which is portrayed as the energy from which the universe is constructed. The duality is born and transforms into Trinity an entirely new and creative unity, from which the universe expands in all its facets by a constant oscillation or alternation of different polarities.

The same way the basic unity of a person splitting sexually manifests in the number Two. Sexuality is in reality only the manifestation for the quantity Two. It is recognized this number represents a thing that has more than a quantifiable nature, but also a purpose, since it is only in relation.

In arithmetic we are only interested in the amount represented by numbers: When the symbol "4" uses, it signifies "four units added together". In geometry, the values are merely ratios. For instance, the term Pi is difficult to comprehend as an arithmetic value that claims to be an unchanging quantity. It is, in essence, the proportion between the circle's circumference along with its radius, with the dimensions of the former being irrelevant. Pi is therefore the purpose of the circle, and the number of the circle being of a strictly qualitative nature.

From the number it has a geometrical shape which means that, in its concrete aspect it's a lot more purposeful or a ratio than it is a number.

This is apparent in the golden ratio. music harmony... In harmony with music there are three pillars of pure and perfect harmony that are the fifth: 2/3 The fourth: 3/4, and the third: 4/5.

Let us go back to the divine and creative Trinity model and the source of all things, as well as preside over everything. The truth is that Trinity is at the root of everything can be evident in these examples The surface, which is the first known form that must possess at least three sides to exist; three primary colors, red, blue, and yellow, are the basis for all other colors; and the life of the animal is dependent on the male, female and offspring, etc.

Furthermore it is true that the Trinity is actually the root of everything. Everything is fundamentally threefold in its structure For instance, man is a person with an body as well as a soul and spirit. The ancients represented these three Principles of all things , namely Sulfur, Mercury and Salt. Each principle is comprised of one of four elements: Fire and Air in Sulfur as well as Air and Fire in Mercury, Air and Water within Mercury as well as Water in Salt, and Water Earth and Earth in Salt. So seven qualitative factors within that make up that is the Three Principles containing the Four Elements. It is important to note that the entire octave of the scale is comprised of seven notes that are pure and light is broken through the prism (triangle) into seven distinct shades.

In actual fact there are seven distinct elements in each phenomenon, and, from these seven elements Harmony is formed. Harmony is the result of the Trinity and is influenced through the four Elements In the sense that it is an effect of the sevenfold manifestations of The three Principles as well as the Four Elements.

Let us not forget this. The Absolute Unity does not create it, but rather divides or splits as it is eternal and invariable. The manifest reality is the split Unity that is it is the Unity that is contemplating it. The One is not able to reproduce, since it is. Procreation is the result of the third dimension. Therefore, all potentialities of the Universe are found in what Pythagoreans described as Tetraktys $1+2+3+4 = 10$.

I

I I

I I I

I I I I

The combination of the numbers that represent the Unique and the polarization of the procreation, and the first form of procreation (the four) creates God the

Divine decade. The numbers are arranged through a triangle, which is the first surface that is possible, meaning that all manifestations occur by the Trinity and is embodied by each of the Four Elements [11 (the three levels within the triangle) to return to the basic Unity because 10 = 1 + 0 = 1.

It is important to remember that nine parts of Tetraktys are organized around one central element, which is the Divine and unintelligible Unit.

Tetraktys Tetraktys represents the metaphysical triangle that is inaccessible to logic. It can be through Trinity which this Universe manifests itself. Therefore by replacing the central , unintelligible Unity by three units that represent the creative basis which is the Ternary We get the Pentactys or to say, the realized Tetraktys.

I

I I

I I I

I I I I

I I I I I

In this case, the original inventive Trinity is enclosed by twelve units. These are the twelve locations of the World which are depicted in the twelve zodiac signs. These twelve units make up the triangle. If we look at them and then count the number of units we can find five units for the base, and three and four for the sides.

It is, therefore, in reality a 3-4-5 triangular that is it is the Sacred Triangle of the ancient Egyptians. In the words of Plutarch: "It seems probable that the Egyptians considered this right-angled triangle to be the most beautiful of all triangles, and that it was to this figure that they compared the nature of the universe." The 3-4-5 triangle formed the basis for the old science of proportions utilized by the builders of the past.

B

A

A I B

A I I B

c c c c c

The twelve units also comprise those of the 12 scale notes, which include the five altered notes i.e. that the twelve notes on the scale of the chromatic, or those of the twelve sixths on the Pythagorean scale. In music, using the sound of 100Hz for the primary note. Note that the note of the octave starts located at 200, with the fifth is at 300 and the next one at 400, three at the 500th. The fifth, and the third make up what is known as the "perfect major chord", according to the ratio 3-4.

Chapter 24: Inexhaustible nature

In addition, according to Pythagoras the soul is composed of a tetrad comprising intellect, science, belief and feeling, from which are all science and art and our own quality of a reasonable being. Aetius, Opinions.

"It it is for the descendants of Pythagoras to inquire what was the view of the Master on this issue as he has never written anything. The person who will be the best to provide us with the information is, in my opinion, Philolaos of Taranto. He begins by writing in a somewhat mysterious manner, in several volumes, the meaning of the world and the significance of each one of them. Then after that, before moving on to the study of the essence in the mind, he dives into a fascinating discussion about the notions of weights, measures and measurements in the fields of music, geometry, and arithmetic. He demonstrates that the entire universe is a result of these concepts. (...)

Let's return to Philolaos who, after we've departed and who in the third volume of his books titled Treatise on Rhythms and Metres speaks of the soul this way"The soul is able to enter the body through numbers and thanks to eternal and inseparable harmony'. He adds: The soul is a lover of the body since it grants the soul access to the senses. After death, it is separated from them from their bodies the soul is able to live an eternal life within the world. Claudian Mamert, On the Soul.

"According to Philolaos, number is the all-powerful, self-generated bond that eternally unites the objects of the world." Jamblicus, Commentary on the Arithmetical Introduction of Nicomachus.

"And in fact, every knowable being has a number: without it, nothing can be conceived, nor known." Philolaos quoted in Stobaeus, Choice of Texts.

"The study of the effect and the core of the number should be done in conjunction with the power of the decade. In fact, the power of numbers is immense infinite, perfect, universal, the basis and guide for the celestial and divine life as well as the human experience and in which it is the strength of the year is a part (missing words included). Without it all things would be inaccessible and a mystery.

The nature of numbers is to every human being a cognizant, instructing and guiding about all things that subject to confusion or ignorance. In fact there is nothing that exist would be apparent to anyone, either by itself, nor in relation to any other thing without the quantity and essence of numbers. It is in fact numbers, by giving all things the same quality to the soul via perception, makes them recognizable and comparable to each other in accordance with what the character of the Gnome is because it is the number that gives them a corporeal appearance and differentiates interactions between things as both unlimited and limited. We can see the nature of number as well as its power of action not just in the realm of divine and demonic as well as in every human action and wordsin all areas and in all the activities of art and in the realm of music." Philolaos quoted in Stobaeus in his the Choice of Texts.

"The early philosophers had right in stating that it is essential to be aware of the measurements that comprise the kairos (the seven) because it is the basis of the philosophy.

Let us employ it to begin the process of explaining the world. If we ensure that we don't slack off our focus, we'll be able do so without the infamous Delphic principle or principles from Strabo, Hestiaios, Archytas, Aristotle and all the writers of maxims of the same type. Athenaeus the Mechanist, Poliorcetics of the Greeks.